A PENN[INE] CHILDHOOD

D0625036

ERNEST DEWHURST

ISIS
LARGE PRINT
Oxford

Copyright © Ernest Dewhurst, 2005

First published in Great Britain 2005
by
Sutton Publishing Ltd.

Published in Large Print 2007 by ISIS Publishing Ltd.,
7 Centremead, Osney Mead, Oxford OX2 0ES
by arrangement with
Sutton Publishing Ltd.

British Library Cataloguing in Publication Data
Dewhurst, Ernest
    A Pennine childhood. – Large print ed.
    (Isis reminiscence series)
    1. Dewhurst, Ernest – Childhood and youth
    2. Journalists – Great Britain – Biography
    3. Large type books
    4. Pennine Chain Region (England) – Biography
    I. Title
    942.8'082'092

ISBN 978–0–7531–9396–9 (hb)
ISBN 978–0–7531–9397–6 (pb)

Printed and bound in Great Britain by
T. J. International Ltd., Padstow, Cornwall

For Renée and our family
for their encouragement and support

Contents

Acknowledgements

I'm indebted to Roy Prenton, editor, and Peter Dewhurst, news editor, of the *Nelson Leader* and *Colne Times* for use of background material on events and on the period from their files and for several archive photographs, and to Peter, my son, who took current photographs of the settings; also to the staff of Nelson Library for access to their newspaper files and to the Independent Methodist Resource Centre for use of its archives.

I've included, with appreciation, several facts from W. Bennett's *The History of Marsden and Nelson* and drawn on the farm aspect from an article I wrote for the *Guardian* newspaper forty years ago. I'm grateful to the Inklings Writers' Group in Liverpool for patient listening and advice, to Jim Bennett for his assessment, to my wife Renée, Geoff and Sandy, Peter and Diane and to Peter Milner who have given encouragement. I value, finally, the example of my great-grandfather, grandparents and parents who laid the foundations for my life and this memoir.

Overture and Beginners

What past can be yours, O journeying boy
Towards a world unknown.

Thomas Hardy

A locomotive, fuelled and watered, stood wheezing and impatient in Bolton railway station. It was the 1850s and the oil-glimmer place was little more than a shed and booking office. The engine, of the Stephensons' period, with open cab and tall chimney, would have carriages varying from padded to painful according to the pockets of patrons and some possibly open to Lancashire rain, with holes in the carriage base to let water out. Class distinction had transferred pompously from road coach to rail and perhaps Sir Osbert Sitwell was justified in his claim that trains summed up "all the fogs and muddled misery of the nineteenth century".

Carriage doors closed with assured thuds. Less assured was the boy, third class, confused, alone, unwanted. In his pocket was a single ticket, a one-way to Colne on the boundary of Lancashire with Yorkshire. Pinned to his jacket was a scribbled label confirming rejection by his stepfather: "ANYONE CAN HAVE THIS LAD THAT WANTS HIM".

The guard's whistle pierced the gloom of boy, station and times. The engine coughed and smoked and shuffled its passengers out of a station which some years before had seen the baptism of the *Lancashire Witch*, a locomotive built by Robert Stephenson. The boy, committed to the unknown with less certainty than a goods parcel, was steaming towards Colne, overlooked by the Lancashire Witch country.

The boy was my great-grandfather and the one-way steaming and the train of events to follow were to colour the outlook of my family and faith into, and through, the twentieth century. The harshness of his Victorian childhood was in harrowing contrast to my own — on a Pennine farm below the empty moors that whispered out towards the Brontë parsonage and the birthplace of Ted Hughes, a future laureate, and above cotton mills, milk rounds and markets, chapels and chip shops, gaslight and gossip, cowboys, comics and classrooms — and all in a dappled clearing between two world wars. The evocation begins in the 1930s and drifts through the Second Darkness . . .

Ernest Dewhurst, 2005

CHAPTER
ONE

Lamp Lighting at Tum Hill

I stood tip-toe upon a little hill . . .
John Keats

Dad farmed on a slope. If I'd lived at Tum Hill for a lifetime I might have developed a slant. The farmyard sloped, the middle field had its tilt and the top pasture bucked and dipped like an unbroken colt as if to indulge its elevated status. It resembled an assault course and may have been one, for it was once part of an Iron Age hill-fort. With its hint of the empty Brontë moors beyond, it could never expect the mowing machine. If mowing had been attempted horse, machine and man could have rolled down towards the house. The bottom meadow was odd. It was flat.

The slopes were no threat to a growing boy founded on milk and eggs. The darkness was. I had never known such darkness. It fell each evening as if some monster had blown out the sun and thrown over us a heavy tablecloth like the one under which we played tents but a million times bigger and with no escape flap. Inside it haunting shapes and figures loomed up like the ghosts on Dad's box camera negatives. The black one watched us through windows and leaned against the door,

1

waiting for Dad to light his storm lamp, go outside and be gobbled up by it. He always came back. The bedside prayers saw to that. Even when stars pinned back the night sky shadowy arms clawed out at me. The glow of oil lamps and coal fire inside the farmhouse could not shut it out entirely, and upstairs, first to bed, I had to have a small lamp and the stairs door left open on the thin gauze of fireside conversation. My fears would linger long, and even in bolder years Dad would post a storm lamp at the top of the short brow to the farm, a lighthouse to wink me home from winter school or Sunday School events.

Winds would howl like wolves up the farmyard, snatching at doors, scattering dogs, cats and buckets and licking up the rainbows of oil leaked into puddles from the milk van. Sheltered in the first years of life in the valley below town, I had never been aware of such gales and expected them to send barn roof, hens and dad bowling off into Yorkshire. But snow was a silent intruder. It came by night, quieter than a whisper, and besieged us inside soft barriers. Looking back, neither blizzards nor gales were too common and were relieved by the armistice of a benign spring giving impartial warmth to cowslip and cowpat. Darkness was different. It called every night, but then everything was black or white to a boy.

The farm was a dozen miles across the Pennines from where the Brontë sisters had imagined their way into world literature over a smoky peat fire. Their moor was in Yorkshire, ours in Lancashire. Somewhere among the becks and cloughs and waterfalls on the weathered fells a change of vowels marked the boundary almost as vividly as stone wall or stream. Our hill was not nearly so bleak or solitary as their wuthering heights, but to a boy shorter than the lower half of a stable door the farm seemed prey to every tantrum of weather even on ours, the lowest rung of the climb. Charlotte, Emily or Anne were not mentioned much in our home. Dad was more absorbed with his lamp-lit keeping of milk and egg records and simply buckling to than the novels of three quaint sisters in a consumptive parsonage, though the subsequent death of one of our relatives from tuberculosis was an echo of their damp times.

Dad had been apprenticed to iron-turning and was a convert to farming. The farm scene had been more in Mother's blood as granddaughter of a farmer and the oldest of six children of a farm auctioneer and valuer who died at forty. Mother and Dad clicked to courtship on their way to different chapels and when I was born lived in Blacko, a hillside village little more than a shepherd's whistle from Yorkshire but enough to give my accent its red rose tinge. The cottage was on an old turnpike where tolls had been charged at a toll house opposite the George and Dragon Inn at Barrowford. At one time a horse passed through for 1d, a horse with chaise for 6d and twenty cows for 10d with a fee for dragons overlooked.

In the year that I emerged, 1926, the world lost Rudolph Valentino and gained Princess Elizabeth. My entry, ginger and whining with a hint of freckles and fidgeting to come, may not have been as conspicuous

3

but I was not held responsible for the General Strike. We moved to Linedred, between river and Leeds and Liverpool canal. From there Dad jingled milk by horse-drawn float with ornate lamps into the Victorian new cotton town of Nelson which owed its name to the old Nelson Inn and, in turn, to the admiral himself. A jalopy with running boards and rooftop sales slogan followed but by the time of Tum Hill Dad had moved up to a small blue van with his name in gold letters on its door. "What yer gooing up thear for? It'll be that cold i' winter." We went and wrapped up. The flitting van, probably the ubiquitous Wesley Clegg's, climbed through town with our belongings in the early 1930s and squeezed along a lane and through the yard of Gib Hill Farm which had more land than us, a milking herd and Irishmen for making its hay. Ours was Little Gib Hill, the farm at the end of the lane, and marked out by that small prefix as junior neighbour. On medieval maps the name may have meant Tom Cat Hill. Whether the removal men saw any tomcats was never made clear but perhaps the grumbling of their gears on that last tight brow by a colour-washed old cottage put them to flight. If Dad had known all the chains and sacks and ashes needed on it in ice or snow he might have himself turned tail and fled with his flitting downhill again. I was glad he didn't.

Gib Hill was one word on old maps and may have referred to the bigger holding of our neighbours, Mr and Mrs Walter Bather and their two daughters; in the seventeenth century a Mr Ridiough kept six cows and fifteen hens on 9 acres there. Dad's land stretched further than a boy could see, even on tiptoe, though some may have dismissed his 14 acres as "nobbut a pocket 'andkerchief of a place". But there for a year or two he was to persevere with hens, a few stirks, a snuffling of pigs and the delivery of another farmer's milk into Nelson with over 30,000 people. The town smoked away between us and Pendle Hill, where a beacon had blazed out the defeat of the Armada and George Fox had a vision before founding the Quakers. We looked across the valley of Pendle Water, a river, to Pendle, which fell short of mountain status by 170ft. If capped, some said, we could expect rain. It seemed fond of its cap. The Tum Hill area was also known as Castercliffe. Our farm, the lesser Gib Hill, was a humble living but it had a soul.

We were a household of four, two parents, an unmarried aunt, Martha, biblical by name and practice, and the one ginger fidget. For one period there was extra help on the milk round and for specials like haytime aunts and uncles would bolster the labour force. The farmhouse had its back to a middle meadow and was tethered to a barn, shippon and stable in line abreast. The small house had a living room warmed by black oven and boiler range, kitchen with stone slopstone and water pump, cool store and bedrooms. Three stone flags from the front and only door gave on to an earth yard and a flagged path hugged the buildings to the bottom gate. The coal shed was handy but the lavatory anything but a convenience. Lavatory was a euphemism for a board with a hole over a short drop and a draughty door with scraps of the *Nelson*

Leader on a nail. It was somewhere down the yard, and paying calls could be a gamble on a foggy foggy night — especially if the newspaper had run out — and it was some relief that chamber-pots were still in fashion.

As with any house removal, and more so to a farm, there was the novelty of settling in with fresh sights, sounds and smells. There was little garden but Mother, who wasted nothing, needed no more than eyes, fingers and scissors to exploit nature — young nettles for nettle beer in spring, wild flowers to deck the home in summer, holly over picture frames for Christmas. In autumn her purpled fingertips and scratched forearms forecast blackberry pie, and if on her searches she chanced on the eggs of a truant hen in grass so much the better. The farmhouse took on a homely smell of its own, our smell, mingling the outdoors, with woodsmoke and paraffin, with whatever was the domestic ritual of the day, Rinso and bubble and squeak on Mondays, baking on Thursdays, furniture polish on Fridays, a timetable rarely altered.

There were times when the nose could have used a peg, like when Mother's hand was inside the reverse end of a chicken, "cleaning it" on the big square table with its heavy tablecloth (mainly for weekends and the eyes of visitors) temporarily removed. I would be engaged in Custer's Last Stand or some Great War attack on my side of the table but there would be no retreat for the general-in-command or later Meccano constructor from that stink of surgery, and the toy farmyard was more in keeping with such table sharing. Outdoor smells could outflank sound or sight and the nose had to be educated into new encounters, from hen pellets and creosote to the patron saint of pong, the Muck Midden, with its dining club no one would wish to hear about. The provender shed smelled almost appetising and grass had seasonal treats for the nose, first when newly cut and then when rafter high in the barn, giving off a fusty, cuddly warmth of which cats, dogs and less domesticated squatters took advantage.

One of Mother's customs was to make a soft cheese and suspend it in a little cloth bag from the slopstone tap, drifting out an acceptable aroma. Baths had to be taken in a tin bath off its peg on a wall and as I bathed, with little enthusiasm, in lamplight by a flickering fire the hot water freed a metallic smell. Sometimes the hearth would be shared with a sickly chick or two on hay in an old hat and, almost inevitably, the wet nose of dog.

I slept at the back of the house. My bed overlooked changes of season in the middle field. Footprints and pawprints in overnight snow did not require Sherlock Holmes to deduce that Dad had been with Towser to feed the pigs. Manure heaps spaced with erratic geometry promised sweet green growth in spring; summer offered swathes of cut grass and, in autumn, leaves would be blown like brown paper bags against the top wall. At times the sky flashed with lightning, then growled with thunder, a barracking that found the ginger head underneath the bedclothes, ears pillowed, praying that the front door had been left open to let the thunderbolt out. None of us had met a thunderbolt so we wouldn't have known what to look for anyway.

CHAPTER
TWO

Parents

Don't be too hard on parents.
You may find yourself in their place.
Ivy Compton-Burnett

The farm was like a draught of spring water to a man who'd served an apprenticeship in the fumes of a town foundry with workmates in wide cloth caps and moustaches like Mexicans in the old westerns. Dad swapped the town fug for upland air but, unlike the foundry, the farm never closed. Between milk rounds he was at work somewhere on the land and a boy could always pester him to mend a bicycle puncture or give advice through a snowstorm of feathers, nails clenched in teeth, the steam bath from stable manure. He was a lean wiry Christian man with the assurance of belt and braces and a khaki smock with big pockets for the milk round. The Protestant faith had invested him with a quiet manner and voice, disciplined workstyle and oath-free language. I caught him out only once in our days at the farm when a barn door trapped his foot and tortured out of him a suppressed "damn".

Dad's belt may have been a threat and, with braces in reserve, was available but it never touched me.

Religion stopped it, I'm sure, though there was no Commandment against a leathering. Conversely, the mild man took to calling me Matey which I accepted as pally enough compared with the copper-knob, carrot-top and "has yer mother left yer out all neet" of the schoolyard. Matey also had a Norsey feel to it and Norse was in some local names.

The family album lived in an old dusty suitcase under a bed and its contents suggested that Dad had patronised an Imperial Studio in the town several times as boy and youth, posing first in broad white starched collar and knee breeches, then with narrow collar and trouser turn-ups and once with thirteen chapel-going male friends uniformly well groomed in suits with waistcoats, polished shoes and partings right, left and centre, all a credit to the faith. It was a group at which Kitchener's finger was pointing largely in vain as most were then too young for dispatch to the trenches though some, including Dad, saw service at home eventually. Those chic portraits of the farmer as youth did not chime in with my image of him later when responsibility and muck without bullets required him to get hands, face and clothes dirty.

He'd worked for a time at a wood yard where one of his duties was to fasten roller skates on to patrons of the firm's rink. With a friend he also dabbled in cycle repairs and was cycling home one night when he fell foul of the law. The constable accused him of riding without a front light and pointed to the alleged offender, one of the old carbide lamps. "It must have just gone out. It was lit when I set out." Dad offered truth from that honest chapel face. "I doubt it, son," the law said, and gave the lamp the finger-touch test of the time. He burnt his fingers.

Though a lifelong abstainer from alcohol Dad had taken to smoking, perhaps in the Army, and developed a habit of docking a cigarette half smoked and pocketing the tab end for further reference. Whether that was his way of saving money or smoking less I never knew but the build-up of nicotine in the butts could not have helped his health in later years. A teetotal lifetime would be borne out by the fact that the only time I would see him walk into a public house would be for water — a canful for an overboiled radiator.

His work in Walton's Foundry fitted him for minor repairs on the farm. His first name was Simpson, after his grandfather, and if called on to hump something heavy like a sack of provender to a hen hut he'd give a chuckle and quip "Hey, my name's Simpson, not Samson." Some might have called him an improviser but many farmers had to be. They would "make do" with odds and ends that lived around the place like heirlooms. "It might just come in handy, that." Some came in handy for my Christmas stocking, a home-made farm or garage perhaps, finished in paint left over from some other job. The family album had the three of us pictured on some promenade with Matey bowling along in a home-made buggy with two wheels and a single handle. Sawn-off bits of wood or broken stones came in for fencing or wall dentistry and as he plugged gaps against the bleak hillside it was a scene frozen in time, the make-do-and-mend of centuries.

The arms of both my parents seemed to be in perpetual motion as if, like the huge mill engines in town, once stopped they would take some starting up again. Hard graft was handed down. When Mother's father died in the second year of the First World War his black-edged funeral card had the melancholy homily:

> Wife and childen shed no tears
> For hard I've laboured many years
> I always strove to do my best
> And now I've gone to take my rest

Sadly, he took his rest at forty, leaving a widow and six children. My mother, Mary Ann, the oldest at fifteen, had to help with the others and graduated in the Protestant work ethic which at Little Gib Hill she was practising further. Sometimes I would see her leave house or outbuilding with arms folded or in apron pockets as if on sabbatical. Much of the time they were plucking poultry, washing eggs, darning, sewing, raking ashes, mucking out, carrying buckets. Ironing had to be done with that inherited tip of spitting on the base of a hot flat iron to test its sizzle against the risk of singeing a petticoat. All the work was done thoroughly, as if for inspection. I, for one, could see no point in ironing handkerchiefs that would be opened up and blown on. By the time of Tum Hill I wiped my nose and tears myself and the trial of inviting me to spit on a hanky to dab facial smudges outside some non-smudge event had been abandoned. Her rite of hand-wetting my hair to smooth it down had a longer life.

Baking day was a weekly outing for nose, eyes and mouth, with rhubarb or apple pie, Quaker Oat biscuits, potato pie, scones and, after school, the honour of licking a spoon after use. Baked batter from flour, eggs and milk at times became Yorkshire pudding, an export to Lancashire which we copied without shame. Sad cake, a currant production, lived down its name by cheering us up. "Can I look?" I'd say, with fingers everywhere. "They look with their fingers i' Bacup," Mother would reply with a pretend tap on the wrist. I never knew why Bacup was so fingered. If a morsel of food fell on to the farmhouse floor she would assure me "it's lost nowt". My worry was whether it had gained anything. Toast was a favourite, especially topped with beans or sardines, signalled by the smell of the toasting fork rite over a red wound in the fire. Bilberry pie was the last act in some moorland excursion with Mother and Dad on hands and knees hunting the purple like bloodhounds in full sniff. Autumn pie-making and jam tomorrow followed prickly assaults on blackberry bushes before the mildew arrived. The plumpest were always out of boy-reach or hidden, but the vision of the jam pan being hauled out of hibernation made up for the scratches and scrubbing out of purple stains from fingers.

Porridge was a winter chest warmer but another "p", prunes and custard, a regular to keep you regular, would be too regular and make my adult years prune-free. Pancakes, tossed or otherwise, appeared on

Shrove Tuesday or, as boys knew it, pancake day. Less appetising in Monday's washday gloom, especially in winter with damp clothes on racks and maidens, was a fry-up of vegetables, survivors from the Sabbath, known as bubble and squeak. It might have sounded like an act on Palace billboards but never really entertained me.

There were some meals that a boy would eat readily until, with time, their slippery secret slipped out and he found he'd been consuming the lining of a cow's stomach. It was called tripe, which suited it. The meal could be eaten cold or warmed with onions. Vinegar would gleam from tiny pockets in the honeycomb type eaten cold, and elder and seam varieties were also on offer; there was some concoction called tripe bits which must have come in cheaper. I remembered Auntie Martha on a tram with a parcel of tripe bits though whether they were for human or animal I easily forgot. Tripe would outlive the tram and had its own following in Lancashire. One of its supporters said it was mentioned by Shakespeare in one of his plays and by Dickens in a novel, which must have given it some sort of status on those market hall tripe stalls and in the cafés dedicated to its cause. Some of us were eating the foot of cow and pig, marked up as cow-heel and trotters, and liver and onions were also on the menu at Little Gib Hill.

Much of Mother's working day was passed in a pinafore but she was amused to hear herself described as "a woman in a clean pinny" in one of my school compositions, which did make it sound as if she sat around all day "doing nowt". I also informed the teaching profession that our hens were not fed in wet weather, which showed an early tendency to fiction writing though even teachers in town would realise that such hens would not survive long in the rainfall shown on their weather maps of Lancashire. Weather watching was important to farmers. "Wind's getting up," Mother would say as if it had been in bed all day. Then Dad would come back from the milk round and say that so-and-so's "got wind up" which meant having fear. Old men would "get wind" and babies "get wind up". As children we had much to learn, not least becoming familiar with that second language. Why, for instance, did it rain cats and dogs and not rabbits and foxes? Rain rain go away, come again another day, we used to chant, but nobody expected a shower of goats and pigs.

At first, gaslight was purring in streets and homes below us in town but we were to live under oil lamps for some time before the big switchover to electricity. Mother's patching and sewing hour was under paraffin lamps with wick and glass; and there was a grander model, an Aladdin lamp with mantle and slim neck, which outshone its cheaper rivals and would never have been given up to Abanazar. Both were centuries brighter than the old rush candles in times when wolves roamed in Trawden forest beyond the hill. For the black outdoors we carried stormlamps with handles and ratchets to raise the glass for lighting the wick. They laughed at some winds, glinting through yard and field like glow-worms, but would surrender to gales. Dad used to take two of them into the old stone pigsty for a night vigil and hang them from a rafter hook or nail to cast flickering shadows over his midwifery with a farrowing sow. It would be some time before a pylon in the top field would rise like a monster behind a family photograph, the obelisk to a new generation, the generation of power, and we would flood the farmhouse with light simply by pressing wall switches, searching every nook and cranny for any speck of dust or dirt. Only with time would we recognise the change from paraffin to power as a labour-saving invention.

Everything about house and farm had contradicted that term and my sparse vocabulary had three dread letters — ING. Most of the jobs calling for what dad called "hard graft" ended in ING — scraping, raking, carting, feeding, watering, muck spreading. Farmers' sons expect to be called on at times and I was a cog, minor and sometimes sluggish, in the labour machine, a pocket money hand to bolster the sales of the *Film Fun* comic and the stop-me-and-buy-one ice-cream pedaller. The cog must have jibbed at times because I'd hear Dad whispering, "he's a bone in his back, that lad". I knew little about bones in backs but all Dad needed to show displeasure was to substitute "that lad" for Matey and, in fairness, I was not all that often recruited — and spending money was assured anyway.

With Auntie Martha as first mate on the milk van much of the housework and some outdoor jobs fell to Mother and much of it was frustrating. The water pump had to be primed with water to make it oblige. If that failed or the pump froze up she had to hump water from a well down the lane, heaving two buckets for balance and having to break the shiny mirror of ice first on crisp winter mornings. Water, humped or pumped, was heated in the boiler of the black range and ladled out with a "lading can" for washing dishes, clothes and humans. It was the job of Mother, together with the sanction of kneeling before the range, auburn head down, to clear ashes, blacklead the monster or damp down the fire with slack and wet *News Chronicles* to keep it in while we were out. "You live on a farm. How lovely that must be." Mother, who like Dad worked long hours without much complaint, would be too loyal to disagree.

As for me, with chronic contempt for washing, I would have been delighted to see the carrying of water made extinct along with such ultimatums as "wash your hands first" and "don't forget to wash behind them ears". Nobody else asked to look behind the ears. I'd outgrown the torment of having all orifices loofahed in the stone slopstone like some baking bowl or pair of overalls. The only consolation from those carbolic rituals was to watch the dirt from my legs whirlpool down the plughole and ask why it always swirled round in the same direction. Water was never far away and mother had found various ways of applying it. Whoever invented water, Matey believed, it could not have been a boy.

CHAPTER
THREE

Stablemates

All animals are equal but some animals are more equal than others.

George Orwell

The farm was a foreign land ripe for exploration and would unveil, season by season as in a children's novel, all its secrets, its hideyholes, creepy corners, cosy haunts, climbs and death-defying downhill rides on wheels or sledge. Before winter had blustered into spring I'd voted the stable as my favourite retreat. That, and one of the spare hen cabins to be used later as a den, were boltholes from "management" though no secret from them. Of all the farm buildings the stable was the snuggest and I believed that Mary and Joseph could have been offered worse. In truth, the main appeal of our stable would be in its trio of successive occupants.

None of the nags of my acquaintance would have earned showground rosettes. Fuzak the donkey was my first personal mount. She may have been the local guest house for fleas and more testing to start up than Dad's petrol engine on damp mornings, but she was all mine. She gave me many a free donkey ride once we could get her on the move. Unlike Dad's van she had no starting handle and it would be with some shame, at least later, that I got her motor cranked in one or two resistant moments with a squirt from a water pistol into one large ear. Dad used to say horses had been domesticated for thousands of years so you'd think in that time someone could have designed something more reliable than a donkey. Again, according to Dad, some of his customers could talk the hind leg off a donkey. I never saw a threelegged one.

"Fuzak. Funny name for a donkey," a school friend said. "Is she from Egypt?"
"Course not," I said. "I think Dad got her in Trawden."
"Sounds Egyptian," he said. "I bet there's lots of z's in Egyptian."

He accepted rides on Fuzak, Egyptian or not, but I had to admit that I'd heard preachers and teachers in Sunday School spouting z names from the Bible and telling about people hopping on and off asses in the holy lands. Didn't Jesus borrow one to ride into Jerusalem before he set about tables full of money and doves? Then there was him with a name like a young sheep, that Balaam whose donkey met an angel with a sword, was beaten for lying down and ticked off its master in a man's voice. Fuzak let out noises from both ends but nothing like words. People used to say you never saw a dead donkey. We did. Fuzak was found d-e-a-d, as Dad spelt it out, behind the stable door one morning, blocking it. Woolly of mind and coat, she was awkward to the end but beloved by man, boy and flea. We didn't give her an Egyptian funeral, whatever that is. Dad said she'd gone to live with Jesus and as asses showed up all over the Bible and Jesus used one himself that seemed the best place for her.

A pony succeeded Fuzak but whether the odd homeless flea booked bed and breakfast on him before he got through the stable door was not known. To school friends he was mine but Dad used him for haymaking and little transport jobs and I borrowed him for riding and for giving town friends flat-cart-tummy. Billy had a temper at times and once took his starter out of my chin when offered oats to catch him in the field. Our dobbins were ridden bareback. There was neither money nor need for saddles. While some boys longed to drive the 4.05 stopping train to Preston, I saw myself in the winners' enclosure talking to King George and his Queen on Derby Day.

"Yes ma'am. We call her Fuzak after a long dead donkey of ours. No ma'am. You don't often see a dead donkey. No ma'am. Funny you should mention that. He wasn't Egyptian. Yes, I can understand that ma'am. You don't have much call for a donkey at the palace. No room in the mews. Too small for the coach."

Gordon Richards was secure and unchallenged. I outgrew the cap size for jockey.

The gentlest and most serviceable of the dobbins to back out of our stable was Jinny, dad's ginger mare. In her time with us she carried the bulk of the manuring, haymaking and general carriage work on her jingle-bell harness, flock-packed collar, chains, hames and carthorse withers. It was Jinny, bless her, who created a curious diversion in our rather routine family day.

We'd lived by the hill for some time when a neighbour's heavy horse got us out of a hole — in the ground. It had been raining without punctuation, not uncommon in the Pennines, and the ground around a sunken well in the middle field had been hoofed into slutch, our name for wet slippery mud. Jinny had gone for one drink too many and was glued into the slutch by suction. Dad mustered the household. No amount of tugging, pushing and blessing the mare would unglue her, and by then she was in some distress. Dad wiped a drip off his nose. Nose drips seemed to visit him when performing unusual or awkward jobs, from cold in winter and sweat in summer. This was a Pennine rain drip and its removal bought a little time for family discussion. "We're doing no good here," Dad said as a second drip explored the end of his nose. "We're all jiggered and asking for a rupture and Jinny's getting cold and jiggered too. Them o'er yonder'll have to help." The words yonder and jiggered were as endemic to dad as nose drips.

Them "o'er yonder" showed up with ropes and muscles and a big and Good Samaritan horse. Muscles on men and horse bulged with the strain and Jinny came out like a forced confession.

Wells and springs were usually a blessing on farms. Sometimes on our family outings in the van we would pass roadside wells and Dad would revive some handed-down anecdote about them. As we climbed the stiff Buckhaw Brow in Yorkshire he would point to an ebbing and flowing well which could fill and dry up without warning. One traveller allowed his horse to drink there and, having turned away to take in the view, found the well was drained dry. He assumed the horse had emptied it and called on a "horse doctor" in Settle for advice. Help was given, the story went, at a cost and locals had a chuckle at the stranger's expense.

On the northern side of Pendle Hill, on a fell road above the attractive village of Waddington, there was a watering hole called Walloper Well. We smiled at the nickname until we heard its supposed origin. A pedlar passing that way overheard a dispute between man and wife and was said to have advised the man that if she was his wife he'd "wallop her well". There were said to be Robin Hood wells on moors on two sides of us but whether the outlaw ever quenched his thirst there was never confirmed to us.

At one time dad provided grazing for two coal horses on his land to help income on a small farm. Their coal yard was opposite my junior school in upper Nelson, and sometimes in summer he would recruit me to ride them home after school. A coal cart served as a mounting block on to one horse and I led the other on its halter up Barkerhouse Road. Perched at such dizzy heights a boy could become a minor hero among classmates, especially if he kept the secret that these were the great softies of the horse kingdom and could have nosed their way to Tum Hill without human help. "Just stick on 'im lad. He'll tek thi to Tum Hill. I bet he con smellt' grass from 'ere. T'other'll foller. They know where they're off to reight enough. A good rest and summat sweet to eat," the coal merchant's man might say through his coal dust mask. The carthorses were wiped off before starting out but some dust must have clung. A girl cousin who went along for a ride on the empty horse got a ticking off for getting her knickers dirty. I could only guess what excuse she'd given at home: "Honest Mum, I don't know how I got a black bottom. I was on a brown horse."

Each morning before the alarm cocks crowed the coalmen were on our field calling softly to the softies. I was never told off or compensated for any black bottoms I might have had but I had animals to thank for extra money once for helping to spread manure on the land. Manure workers somewhere in the district got a rise in 1936 but I didn't notice much improvement in my pay. Still, I was years better off than boys who were pushed up chimneys or were paid tuppence a day to scare rooks from cornfields with wooden clappers.

Farmers used to help each other out. Dad's friend near Pendle Hill borrowed Jinny and I was called on to ride her home again, via the blacksmith's forge in town which catered for horses and machines used in industry and agriculture. The blacksmith was a lure for boys. The glow of the furnace, pumping of bellows, the hiss of steam, shooting stars and ring of steel on iron was a firework show for all the senses. The man was an artiste, lifting the huge fetlocks to his apron, shaping and punching and filing and fitting the shoes, quenching tools with a sausage pan sizzle and spitting out his steel teeth to pin on the shoes. We sniffed the burning hoof, Jinny and me. She didn't seem to flinch. "Don't worry lad. She doesn't feel a thing and just think what a grand clatter her new shoes'll make trotting up Hallam Road. They'll hear her coming all reight."

I remembered the horses with warmth, the leisurely giants with fetlocks like hens, the wily little pony with his moods and the donkey with its brakes on, both on dainty hooves. I loved their nuzzlings and habits, the sidelong looks in their eyes, the smell of their coats and oats and harness and even the pungent ammonia of their outgoings, the least offensive of all farm manures. Our cattle were so much splashier in their number twos and could surprise a naive onlooker from a couple of yards away. Someone worked out that a cow could part with 7 tons of dung a year, a statistic of distinct interest to dung beetles and dung flies, patrons of Café Cowpat. We called them cow claps, clapping being suited to delivery, and found them tolerable only when dry. Matey acquired some notoriety for scooping up dry claps and hurling them towards visiting girls to show off, a vulgarity unlikely to have founded competitive cowpat throwing in this country.

CHAPTER
FOUR

Callers

Lift the farm like a lid and see
Farm within farm and in the centre, me.
Norman MacCaig

In midwinter we had our paths almost to ourselves.
First footprints on a crop of snow would be ours and
the cry "it's sticking" would bring a frown to Dad
and a buzz to me. Sledges appeared and the steepest
run for visiting school friends was down a neighbour's
field with the gamble of an icy stream at the bottom.
"Dare yer lad. Bet yer'll go in." "It's nowt, but mi
mother'll kill me if I get soaked. Laiking in that beck
again." From Good Friday on, the hill and approaches
were open season and in summer townspeople came
up with haversacked sandwiches, Smith's crisps with
elusive salt bags and Haworth's sarsaparilla, dark,
refreshing and hard to spell. Children roly-polied
downhill into cowpats, played tig and Lone Rangered
with two-finger gun muzzles and the ker-ker-ker of
fire. "It's not fair, Mum. He won't lie down. He's bin
dead twice, he has." Old men boiled up the brow,
buttressed by walking sticks and younger arms to
bird's-eye view the valley between Nelson and Colne,

reassembling the jigsaws of youth, reminiscing about missing pieces.

Mothers and grandmothers came, squeezing through stiles tighter with time. Dogs growled at ours; ours growled back near some emergency exit. Youths swaggered up in leg-pull cliques, daring each other to pass sulky cows which might just be bulls. The superstitious heard the cuckoo and turned over money, if they had any. Calf lovers climbed, smouldering. On parched evenings with sap rising like mercury the hillside hollows were summer's back seats at the pictures. Men whom Dad called "grasshoppers" spied through field glasses at cuddling. The town had few corners from which the countryside couldn't be seen and to trade a cobbled street for a benign hilltop was a bargain worth striking. At the farm we had our callers even though in summer they could be conscripted to make hay. An only child, I envied classmates who played with brothers or formed little gangs in streets. From one old picture even girls had gangs. On it were six girls and a boy with the caption "Our Gang" and the word "Chips", though whether that was its name or hopes for a back-yard supper was unclear.

I'd begun to attend St John's Junior School next to its church in the upper town. Education had its baptism in the lower town but time erased like a blackboard duster details of it. A photograph of a woman teacher, smiling, with "our class" at Whitefield School achieved only partial success in naming faces. George Lancaster, my new head at St John's, had his own evocations of boyhood. He used to take two tame mice into class in his pocket and once, sorry to say miss, a tame rat. These, he'd say on retirement later, would frolic on his desk while teacher was writing on the board and he pocketed them when she turned round. Perhaps that was why he understood children and said they must be allowed to "let off steam" at times. Whether any pets frolicked under his regime was unknown to me but ours were too big for pockets and even his steam allowance wouldn't run to a ginger horse clumping between desks.

Friends from there, and secondary school to come, would jolly up to the farm for flat-cart jaunts behind Billy or downhill on wonky wheels imitating Campbell's record of 300 mph at Utah. "A ticklish moment," he said of a burst tyre at 290, and became a pin-up. Less graphically, we played marbles, ate sugar butties, swapped cigarette cards and comics, rattled ball bearings on a home-made bagatelle, sat on buckets, walls or sacks of hen pellets and gossiped like little old men. Perhaps we made bows and arrows in territory where centuries before every male from child to sixty had compulsory archery practice, usually on Sunday. The Sabbath? The grandmas would have frowned on that.

Boys went home with brambled legs, cow muck stains, dog-haired, dirty, tired and late with pink cheeks and hillside hunger. None could report unearthing Roman coin, cannon ball, a flint, fly-past or off-course Pendle witch. None were for our times though boys may once have played out in some fear of spectral horseman, ghost of Victorian child, monk with handless wrist, witches, boggarts bogeymen, all alleged historically or hysterically within an hour's pony ride from us. The most bizarre was a wretched cat in Trawden village beyond the hill, said to have been bounced as a ball by youths to vanish in a blinding flash, never to be seen again, and who could blame it? Sometimes gypsy women would call with hand-made pegs in a basket and I used to like to see gypsy caravans on grass verges outside town, pots on fires, smoke-faced children and sturdy cobs caught by well-weathered men by their shaggy manes. Perhaps Dad longed for a taste of their travelling life. He promised himself to hire a horse-drawn caravan to clip-clop through Ireland on holiday. It would never happen.

If we'd wanted Romans or witches we'd have had to invent them. There were two girls at the next farm whose friendship I would never have risked by asking them to play at casting spells or boiling frogs' legs. An occasional playmate stayed at his grandmother's cottage. Gran was a wiry woman who sold biscuits. Her husband, a dour retired man of eternal silence, scratched away at a small plot. I imagined some dreadful Great War wounding of his voice box. Then one winter's afternoon I arrived at the end of our lane in a snow flurry. The mute man loomed up, black against white and dusted with snow: "Walk behind me, lad," he said. I walked in his wake, a trawler sheltered by a liner, and saw him afterwards in a warmer light.

We hadn't lived there long when I found, on one of my apprentice explorer days, that the path up our middle field dipped into a gloomy, creepy depression and led on a track to a farm underneath the summit of the hill. There I met two Bills, young Bill, a boy, and Big Bill, a horse and a half. Both had long hair. The boy called his a "winter coit" but seemed to wear it at all seasons as he visited us. Old Bill I reckoned was the tallest and most ancient of Shires and could at one time have pulled over the town hall but in my time was creaking and, as remembered, slept upright in bellybands.

Uncles and aunts came, honorary haymakers, among them Uncle Cecil, with Annie, my mother's youngest sister and former May Queen of Barrowford village, borne to her reign in robe and crown and open-top car of the 1920s. White again for her wedding to Cecil and, though fidgeting was allowed, a few prayers must have gone up when she invited Matey, aged a tiresome eight, to be page boy. Pages were for palaces and the prospect of me cushion-bearing without mishap was almost beyond belief.

Though Mother's side would give me ten cousins, in time there were then just four of us in minor roles. Me and my donkey fringe were in silk shirt and trousers which swept the pavement, buttonholed and bearing a tasselled cushion to hold something very ceremonial. Cousin Marian was in long dress and cousins Joyce and Sidney, also in white, held hands for support at the greatness thrust upon the very young. The bridal pair, members of a gospel mission, were semi-circled for one photograph by women in the smocks, bows and black berets of their cause, each with Bible.

28

Uncle Emmott, Mother's brother, with his wife Ethel clinging to him on the pillion, would come spluttering up on his AJS motor cycle wearing a sailor cap with peak and white top, and made Matey's flesh creep with spooky tales about Dracula and Frankenstein and creepy old actors like Lon Chaney and Boris Karloff. By then I'd forgiven or forgotten one of his specials when I was table-top height and he made his seasonal entry into the gaslit living room of Grandmother's house in a borrowed Father Christmas outfit. I was unrehearsed for the red cloak and white beard of the stranger of Ford Street. One glimpse of red in the gloom and the tears flowed. The moral was that for house calls to small customers the Christmas giver should be anticipated and thanked but not seen.

Uncle Emmott took me on summertime scary rides on his motor cycle, which seemed all tubes and spokes as if assembled by Meccano set, and when hurled at hump-backed bridges it felt as if the bolts would come out. Emmott and Ethel had no children but their home offered a "good read" for a boy, especially the story of three supermen, Longshanks, Girth and Keen, whose physical powers were outstandingly useful. My aunt and uncle were *Daily Express* readers, which gave me my first sighting of the Nutwood comic strip character in check trousers and scarf, Rupert Bear. Uncle played a successful game of billiards. He would drift eventually into farming and once, when we'd overlooked milk for tea for a family picnic, he would roll up his trousers and wade into the shallows of a lake to milk one of several browsing cows which were tail-flicking flies and too contented to move away. I often used to imagine the dialogue if this cameo of an unorthodox milking parlour in some other setting had come to court:

Chairman of Bench:	And where exactly did this milk come from, officer?
Constable:	From a cow, your worships.
Chairman:	I know it was from a cow. But what was the milk in when it was taken?
Constable:	In the cow, sir.
Chairman:	I don't think you quite understand the question, officer. I'll ask you again and you may consult your notes if your memory is faulty. Where precisely was the milk?
Constable:	The milk was in the cow. The accused milked it from the cow.
Chairman:	You mean . . .
Constable:	. . . Yes, your worships. The milk was in the cow and accused milked the cow thus purloining it.
Chairman:	I see. The milk was taken from the cow's . . .
Constable:	. . . udder, sir.
Chairman:	Just what I was about to say. From its bladder. And where was this cow at the time of this strange offence?
Constable:	In the lake, your worships.

Chairman:	Is he pulling our legs, Mr Clerk? Or is he not feeling too well? Perhaps he should get some air.
Clerk:	No, your worships. He is correct. The milk was in the cow and the cow was in the lake.
Chairman:	Don't tell me. The accused was in the lake too.
Clerk:	Yes sir.
Chairman:	And I suppose the cow jumped over the moon.
Constable:	No sir, the moon wasn't out. It was broad daylight.
Chairman:	Well, that's more than I'm seeing — daylight. Case dismissed for lack of daylight. Next case.
Clerk:	Drunk in charge of a donkey, your worships.
Chairman:	Let me guess. The donkey was in the lake too.
Clerk:	No, your worships. In the lane.
Chairman:	Thank goodness for small horses.

And they wouldn't make them for ever, AJS motor cycles and Uncle Emmotts.

CHAPTER
FIVE

The Shining Hour

And the Sabbath rang slowly
In the pebbles of the holy streams.
Dylan Thomas

Sunday was different and the difference could be heard. A hush graced the smokeless town and the day was largely fenced off from the week like a field being rested and in the spirit of Genesis — God blessed the seventh day and sanctified it. Non-believers probably called it dead and breathed into it what life they could. Believers isolated it. Even on the farm where a day of rest suggested famine for livestock the work would be pruned to feeding and watering with time allocated for family worship, with hens clucking relief for a temporary armistice and no Sabbath semaphore of washing on the clothes-line, though the command to the Israelites not to light fires on that day was overlooked.

Whatever else, I would be washed and brushed and manoeuvred into Sunday best and taken to Sunday School with coppers for the collection, a hint to be good and the thought that I was presentable on leaving home at least, a link with the notion that clean underpants should always be worn in case of accident. Perhaps the money burned a futile hole in the pocket because it couldn't be spent even if a shop could be found open on a 1930s Sabbath.

Chapel-going was a handed down rite for many families and in ours that faith and practice had had a poignant nudge in the 1850s when a train sneezed out of Bolton for Colne. Its most confused and lonely passenger was a boy with a label pinned to his jacket which read "ANYONE CAN HAVE THIS LAD THAT WANTS HIM". He was my great-grandfather. He was born on a farm near Colne to the biblically baptised Isaac and Kezia. After they both died the boy found himself living with a stepfather and drunken stepmother whose home was in Bolton. In her alcoholic turmoil the woman put him out into the street without clothing and he was taken in overnight by a sympathetic neighbour. At the age of eight he was bundled off to a textile mill to work as a doffer and in that bleak and arduous atmosphere he was found to be fainting repeatedly from need and harsh treatment. So it was that the stepfather, assuming the boy would become a drain on family finances, took him to Bolton railway station, labelled and with a one-way ticket like a goods parcel. Was there at best a flicker of warmth in pointing him towards his birthplace? Back in Colne he was "adopted" by relatives and repaid them by nursing invalids and working on the farm. Out of curiosity he found his way at the age of twenty into the Cloth Hall in Colne and heard earnest appeals from an eccentric evangelist, Fiddler Joss. Salvation was delayed until, on his way home, he prayed on his knees in an outbuilding at Birchenlea Farm. "His soul flamed with light," the writer of his obituary notice would recall.

The boy, Simpson Dewhurst, went on to be a teacher, preacher and Bible class leader at Salem Independent Methodist Church in Nelson, and laid one of the foundation stones of its new building in 1891. The faith and influence of the bearded Simpson continued through my grandfather John Henry, my father, Simpson, and found me, the next generation, in Salem Sunday School, perched on a small chair in a pleasant room with a sloping glass veranda behind Montague Burton Ltd, the tailors. The room was the primary department where chairs, wash-basins and lavatories were childsize and cloakroom hooks at infant eye level like a set for Snow White and the Seven Dwarves. The woman leader had elevated status behind a table as the pianist jollied us into jaunty hymns and choruses. Shiny words lit our time there. "Jesus bids us shine." "All things bright and beautiful." "Jesus wants me for a sunbeam." "God make my life a little light." Sunday School was a cosy, safe and bright place to be. At some point the collection box was taken round to wind up the dropping of coins on the wooden floor, a cadence giving point to the jingle "Hear the pennies dropping", which partnered the collection. Older infants drew chairs into circles for teaching. Toddlers were led like the Israelites to a brown wilderness, a sandpit with scooping toys where some would have buried coins as treasure if they hadn't been parted from them first.

The Almighty entered our lives at birth through the Cradle Roll and in my infancy teachers used to go round knocking on the doors of non-members to "claim" new babies for the Roll. Happily for me the christening ceremony that followed in our chapel was more sprinkling than Anglican waterfall of baptism. Some children were offered the Christian message in Sunday school, others in weekday school assemblies or in homes like that of my grandma Hargreaves who felt obliged to remind callers that "Jesus is Head of this House" above the fireplace and had a promise box of scrolls from which we were encouraged to draw out and unroll a text, a sort of scriptural bran-tub — "Thy words were found and I did eat them", Jeremiah 15, 16.

At Christmas each department of Sunday school had its own party where the dog in a game called "The Farmer Wants a Wife" was apt to get an unchristian pummelling. London Bridge could fall heavily on certain fair ladies and we played musical chairs, hats and mats and the curiously named Dree Dro Dri Droppit in which a handkerchief mimicked a pigeon. Sandwiches and jellies were available for small mouths and suddenly the leader would let out a long hissing SSSSHHHHHHUSH. "What can you hear, children?" What we could hear was a bell which we were all ready to accept was the jingling trademark of the man from Lapland as he reindeered over Pendle Hill, around the centre clocktower and down on Montague Burton's flat roof. Perhaps we carolled him in and there was always a communal gasp when the door opened and there he stood, a church officer, preferably round-faced, disguised as Father Christmas, trying to look genuine and anxious that some precocious child would not rumble him and call out, "It's Mr Barrett. I know his boots", dismantling the deception for a generation. Some faces hid in bosoms, some tears leaked out but none would have missed that magical moment. The baby in the crib might symbolise the greatest gift to the world but the man with the sack had the one we could take home.

We quickly discovered a spooky spiral staircase rising to backstage in the main school hall, designed for "artistes and fire escape". No small child dared its gloom alone but bravely climbed it nose to heel with others, thrilling to each ghostly twist to be hushed into the wings of the stage for children's Sunday afternoon presentations for audiences of child encouragers. Themes were spelt out in huge letters on cards reversed on given signals by card carriers. A child with a letter upside down could achieve the snigger and sympathy of the afternoon. I wasn't lettered, perhaps for that reason and risk, but was placarded "Boy Wanted" once with a moral poem to declaim. In a large Sunday school the competition for speaking parts was keen. The King's English was scarcely endemic in north-east Lancashire and I was enrolled for elocution lessons with a Mr Birrell. As I would be hailed as a Mancunian years later in the Royal Navy I assume Mr B got me no closer to Buckingham Palace-speak than that northern city.

Chair sizes grew with age, through Junior and Intermediate (secondary school age) to adult classes when the sexes parted company, the men on raffia chairs in one room, the women in another on soft stand chairs and graduating with age to armchairs and sofas. Grandma seemed to have been forever sofabased.

I was never sent for mouth organ lessons but got into the back row of a mouth organ band conducted by Mr Burrows. We were only a tissue closer to the Hallé Orchestra than comb and paper bands and it was a miracle that dads could be prised away from winter firesides for multiple wheezing. One expert said the mouth organ was in direct descent from the pan pipe and blowing was good for health, a claim which may not have been shared by one adjudicator who had to listen to "Annie Laurie", a test piece, one hundred times. I never managed to master those harmonicas with sliding parts and must have been included more for my singing than Larry Adlerism. I specialised in "Love's Old Sweet Song", which seemed old and sentimental enough to have encountered Queen Victoria, and began

> Once in the dear dead days beyond recall
> When on the world the mists began to fall

and moved into a lump-in-the-throat chorus, "Just a Song at Twilight". Perhaps the doors were locked before the mists, twilight and tears began to fall.

At various levels of Sunday School and in chapel services we used to sway-sing "Tell me the stories of Jesus" with its waltz rhythm, and over time were told and retold the stories. We'd be off into the mountains with that shepherd to look for his lost sheep, and gloom

37

around with a woman by candlelight for a misplaced coin. Parables, they were called. Some children would be more alert for the miracles and anxious, the first time at least, to hear whether Jonah got out of the whale, Daniel out of the lion's den and those chaps with tongue-tying names out of the fiery furnace — all of which made a bit of help with multiplication tables seem a minor request. God was love, we learned from pulpits and wayside pulpits, and felt that a God who could arrange for trumpets to blow down walls and feed a football-sized crowd with a few loaves and fishes would have no trouble looking after us in the dark. Perhaps as a farmer's son I found special interest, also, in the stable birth with unspellable gifts from wise men, probably teachers, and shepherds who seemed to watch over their flocks more carefully than the one who lost a sheep, and that great ark with two-by-two animals trooping into it. Imagine trying to get two Fuzaks up the gangplank, and without water pistol too.

Ultimately churches came together once a year for the Whitsuntide Walks of Witness when it seemed that half the town walked and the other half watched. Banners and bands hyphenated churches and chapels, and banner-bearing was a rite of man, with girls recruited on the ropes. Men carried the poles of the big banners in metal cups and a gust of wind could send an agonising message to the groin. Carriers would have been forgiven for some agnosticism to the text about the yoke being easy. Males reached a kind of manhood under the poles. Some claimed it with first trilby, sneaked Woodbine or candid love affair but some dated their maturity to that banner ritual. Once, our chapel walked bannerless. The fabric had ripped.

Sadists knew where to stand as parsons, drums and banners blew down Bradley Road, the windiest slope. The procession formed from side streets into the river of witness — elders, Sunday Schools, Scouts, Guides, infants on decorated coal carts, women in spring hats, men in bowlers with umbrellas in a pointed reserve on faith in the weather. Volunteers had been recruited for brewing coffee, ordering buns and washing mugs, before, on the day and afterwards, and the faithful relaxed with bun and coffee and a field day to follow. After egg and spoon, three-legged, sack and other races another man with a sack appeared, the official toffee thrower who rained boiled sweets and caramels for a scramble of children.

Was it after one of these walkabouts that mischief went to the head, literally? The bowler hat still adorned some of our men, a target for snowballs, but one day targeting went further. Bowlers on hooks in the gentlemen's cloakroom were mysteriously switched around. The switchers would be well clear when hat-gathering came but the reaction was perhaps something like this:

"Hey. This is no'an my hat, Jim," from the tall man with a 6 on a size 7 head.
"Pea on a drum, this'n brother."
"No, and this 'ere isn't mine, Billy," from a short man with a bowler over his ears. "It's gone that dark."

39

★ ★ ★

There must have been some sort of inquest unless, of course, the culprits managed to keep it all under their hats.

Attendance at Sunday School was probably never questioned by children. It was as much a ritual as washing behind the ears and, for my part, much more welcome — especially as there were prizes available. The going rate when I was eleven was two shillings for a first prize, for 90 per cent attendance, and one shilling for a second, for 80 per cent. As we would hymn our way upwards through Sunday School to those raffia chairs for men and the plush ladies' lounge few of us could have predicted the impact it would have on our lives. The movement was woven into the fabric of the mill towns, as elsewhere. Our main school hall was linked by covered bridge to the cavernous chapel, a symbol perhaps of bridge-building between school and chapel, to fill some of the 900 pews. Even allowing for the darkness to come in the Second World War, some would stay on to work in the chapel or other churches. Others would leave for university and worship elsewhere. Some, more inclined to the social and sports life of Salem, would drift away, but they were never to forget the friends and fellowship and foundation laid there.

CHAPTER
SIX

Boy

Laughter . . . the most civilised music in the world.
Sir Peter Ustinov

The village of Blacko, pronounced Blacker by some, dawdled uphill on the Red Rose side of the turnpike road to Yorkshire. Blacko Tower stood sentinel over it, the legacy of Jonathan Stansfield, a grocer, who had hoped to peer into Ribblesdale from the top but was disappointed. His folly was not to be confused with an ancient Malkin Tower where at dead of night with winds howling and owls shrieking witches were said to meet, and even in more informed times some believed that beads or a chain on a baby's wrist would thwart their influence.

Blacko Independent Methodist Chapel, my mother's childhood Ebenezer, stood by the turnpike with its back to the tower and offered the opposite of evil. Her childhood home was a farm down the village and the cottage of my birth was within earshot of the chapel's hymn singing on its best attended days. Later, from Tum Hill, we would travel to sample there, and at other chapels, the Jacob's Joins or Faith Teas where the faithful found the food and the organisers had faith that it would go round! Such feasts began with a sung Grace which the faithful knew by heart and strangers and boys mouthed self-consciously without sound. Graces varied, but a common one was John Cennick's four-liner:

> Be present at our table Lord
> Be here and everywhere adored
> Thy creatures bless and grant that we
> May feast in Paradise with Thee.

Blacko Chapel would offer a splendid "do" at times, with snowy tablecloths concealed under home-made sandwiches, cakes, jellies and other temptations for boys, and tea urns steaming like locomotives. The meal was laid out in the basement schoolroom and after the crockery was washed, dried and stacked the tables were cleared, benches arranged and the entertainment began. Children were ushered to the front for uninterrupted viewing and it was there one Saturday evening that two comics sold silk stockings from a market stall. One held up the hosiery and joked about it. Nothing unseemly, of course, for chapel ears. The voice, light and squeaky and full-blown Lancastrian, would pipe across the nation in years to come. The stocking spieler was the young Jimmy Clitheroe, cutting his thespian teeth in his Sunday School.

James Robinson Clitheroe was to join the Winstanley Babes and appear in northern theatres. On stage at the Palace Theatre in Nelson in 1937 he would play an accordion as big as himself and wouldn't forget the home village nearby, and take seventeen chorus girls to tea with a Mrs Jay in Blacko. According to contemporary reports they would climb to see Blacko Tower and sip the waters of a never-failing spring at Spout Houses, said to be good for the complexion. That Christmas Eve Jimmy reached sixteen but would remain the perpetual schoolboy, chirping Lancashire from stage, radio, film and television. (Nobody knew the spring waters were so effective.) Fifteen million were to listen to the Clitheroe Kid and his catchphrase, "Some mothers do 'ave 'em", on the wireless.

Many churches and chapels of the time were spiritual and social centres offering Saturday evening entertainment as an alternative to commercial shows and plays. Nothing harmful. Correctness and innocence survived long but it was in that hillside chapel at Blacko where I experienced an early rite of passage of sorts when a woman aired her motherhood, not on the stage in that sweet hallowed place but in the backroom women's world of clatter, plates and patter where no male above a naive and sheltered eight had gone. Rite of passage for a boy, a glimpse of a baby being breast-fed. A time to blush.

CHAPTER
SEVEN

Rosycheeks

The cow is of the bovine ilk
One end is moo, the other milk.
Ogden Nash

Of all our livestock the cows were the most inquisitive.
Set out a picnic or line of washing and their long blank
faces would appear. One summer evening the chapel
choir was invited to the farm and in the warmth of
weather and occasion the choirmaster decided it would
sing for its supper and in the open air. Salem Choir at
the time was a tour de force in quantity and quality,
and its farmyard crescendos must have sent a
palpitation of small birds and beasts hurrying to sky or
cover with a hallelujah deafness. You could almost hear
the mice complaining: "What a racket. Why doesn't he
just trap us or leave us to take our chances with the
cats? That contralto'll be the death of us or that deep
bass. Death by booming."

Not so the cows. With them the opposite occurred.
Accustomed only to the sawmill of bees, the gossip of
small birds and their own crunching of grass they
approached the yard song by degrees to investigate the
damage. Whether they supplemented the mezzos or

baritones or gazed in silence, inscrutable, is lost in time. One soprano, more in tune with anthems than appendages, insisted they were all bulls and feigned fear. Whatever the small creatures of the yard heard was not minuted, but the season was not suited to "the cattle are lowing".

Our cattle were not on sophisticated production lines. Science was still tethered largely in towns and ours was an earthy animal kingdom. Someone, perhaps one of my more bookish aunts, told me that a Mister Holbrook in a novel called *Cranford* had "six and twenty cows" named after letters of the alphabet. If we'd gone for lettering in the shippon we'd never have got beyond the letter G most of the time. Who could imagine a stirk called G. Our herd, a breathtaking overstatement, could usually be counted in on one hand. Only one was ever a "milker". Stirks were christened on arrival and remembered long after they left. Rosycheeks and Rosie had red markings against white and pointed to a lack of imagination in our baptismal process. Dad kept only young stock and bought and sold animals usually in the Yorkshire market town of Skipton, a 14-mile drive away, which held auctions on Mondays. Farmers went to the mart and wives to the street market. Both had an eye for bargains.

At the mart the rural scene was unloaded into manured and marketable movement. "Four broad teeth and four little 'uns!" A chopped forest of sticks came in for leaning on, pointing with and hurrying up bewildered animals out of their natural element. I

45

relished the gossiping and bargaining voices of farmers in Lancashire and Yorkshire dialects with the falsetto cry of the auctioneer reaching the high notes. Under a canopy of skewed caps and tobacco smoke the bids came through winks, nods, raised fingers or sticks and, in theory, if you picked your nose you could be knocked down for a heifer in calf. The auctioneer's fast delivery could have bowled out Lancashire. Dad's face would signal whether the price was right and he could have been forgiven at times for muttering that the only good thing to come out of Yorkshire was the road to Lancashire. None of our cattle were classy enough for exhibition as those of the pedigree men. None of your Castercliffe-the-Third, Little-Gib-Griselda or Tum Hill Pride-of-the-Pennine-Dairy for our ruminants whose only publicity beyond the pasture would be on the edge of a family photograph and only noticed on developing. "Hey, look dad. You've got a cow's head on thear." So what, it was a farm. There had, however, been one of that ilk in a village beyond Colne which made the newspapers and a picture-frame on the wall of a local public house, and was still fresh in the memory of my parents.

In the summer of 1912 the cow, having perhaps imbibed too liberally at the pub, fell into the Leeds and Liverpool Canal at one end of a tunnel in Foulridge. The tunnel was nearly a mile long and before barges were hauled through by steam tug they were walked by professional "leggers", on their backs pushing against the walls. The barge horses walked round with their handlers. As for the cow, having no knowledge of geometry or geography, it splashed out for the semi-circle of light at the opposite end and was revived with alcohol, giving birth two weeks later to a calf. The cow got its mile certificate but nowt for common sense. I expect we'd have called the calf Lucky. Humans were less lucky. Some years later a motor-boat captain chugged through the tunnel without permit and was fined £2 17s. I was eleven when the tug service was made redundant by engine power on barges.

There was no deep water for our cows to fall into but one of Dad's nightmares was the escape of animals through gates left open by walkers. A family posse would be organised to hunt down absconders, cattle usually, on lanes above the top pasture. "Needs a spring, you gate," he said. I never saw one.

Tongue-twisters like artificial insemination and animal husbandry were on lips in laboratories but never heard on local farms or among the winks and oaths of auction marts. A bull was a bull by gum and nothing artificial about him, seeing to his own harem and guests from the herds of less prosperous farmers. It was almost a ritual, the serving of cow by bull, and tomorrow's milk and beef depended on it.

Apart from horses, cattle and hens and my special phobia, the spider, the farm had a pig or two, two dogs and a mewing of cats. We were sheepless except for Larry the Lamb, courtesy Uncle Mac on BBC's *Toytown* with Mr Grouser and Ernest the policeman. ("Mr Mayor sir. Did you eat all the sausages?"). Towser and her son Prince were mongrels but pampered like pets. We had few cows to round up and the canines, being more schemers than ratters, delegated pest control to the cats and occupied the roles of doorstep and hearth ornaments. Dad's two-finger whistles, which any Yorkshire Dales shepherd would have envied, was blown more to call me in from play than to work the ornaments. I tried the whistle using various fingers but never mastered it, for which the family was thankful. Only with years did it dawn on me that as I tumbled around the fields with our dogs I was within a horse ride of moors where Emily Brontë drew inspiration from walks with Keeper, her mastiff, which followed her slim coffin to Haworth Church. Names like Harbour Hill, Withens, Sladen Beck and Rushy Clough must have caught the imagination of the parsonage sisters on their walks among heather, becks and waterfalls.

We only had the creepy hollow (my name) for inspiration and it was near there that Dad kept one or two pigs in a stone building, often housebound, pigs being allergic, they said, to cold and sun. They led a rather sheltered indoor life, snoozing and snuffling in the trough with access in suitable weather to an outdoor pen. Farmers used to say that everything about the pig except its squeak could be used, pork, bacon and ham for meals, bristles for brushes and skin for hides. As ours rolled about in mud, sometimes, it seemed impossible to accept that they were more intelligent than horses or cows.

For one period we kept two goats. "Save mowing," somebody probably joked. One of these shaggy creatures had to be milked and one memorable day I undertook the rite before going to school. Close contact was demanded and close contact with Matey in school that morning was largely absent. The reaction was perhaps something like this:

Phew. Who's that?
Not me.
Not me.
Nor me, lad.
Bet it's coming from t'toilets.
More like gasworks, lad.
No, it's nearer than that.
That's no stink bomb. It's Dewi.

Bucketing the night soil from the hens ranked high until I milked the family goat.

Vets must have supplied Dad with various remedies for common complaints in cows, horses or hens and something for fleas on dogs, cats or donkey but what would be remembered more was one heartbreaking service to us when Towser, much loved mother of young Prince, had to be *put down*, as the second language had it. Put down was common enough but because we'd learned what it meant the phrase had a chilling ring, even for adults.

Then there was the lion. Or was there? Did I imagine the lion? Robbie Hayhurst, whose posters billed him as "The World's Greatest Trick Cyclist", used to rehearse his death-defying act on a field near us. To boys the world's greatest anything was a sure draw and unknown to the death-defier he had, at least once, an audience of one watching him dare to defy it. I would spy from a wall as he set his special machine on a slow steady course across a flat field and climb the eight-rung ladder rising above it. Other breathtaking death defying would follow. One day some boy claiming to be in the know told me that Robbie had a lion as pillion passenger when he rode a wall of death in a crackle and whiff of exhaust fumes on summer fairgrounds. How I hoped for that wild beast to show up on our local meadow. That would have been something for the class, the king of the jungle on a motorbike in Nelson. Sadly, nothing fiercer than a tomcat or two showed up. A more sceptical mate said if Robbie had a lion behind him in his act it would have rubber teeth and claws and be well drugged. I didn't care. I'd still like to have seen that big cat riding pillion on our local grass, rubber or real. It was little consolation to pass the entrance gates to Marsden Park below our lane and see two lions there, stony-faced creatures, one on top of each entrance pillar, stone dead and as exciting as algebra.

CHAPTER
EIGHT

Thespian Hens

A hen stares at nothing with one eye,
then picks it up.

Norman MacCaig

In misty dawns with bats and day birds changing shifts
and tiny creatures grateful for a snoozing owl the
cockerels undertook the early morning calls. We took
no risks and set our own alarm clocks but overnight
visitors, accustomed only to the clog and clip-clop of a
stirring town, heard the crowing most and in the
stillness could be disturbed by cattle cropping grass.

From the ratio of poultry to other stock ours was
often called a poultry farm. I did a fair impression of a
clucking hen because I lived, breathed and ate chickens.
A mathematical misfit in school I might have earned a
few feathers in the cap if a question had started "take
ten hens . . .". I was never asked to spell Wyandotte or
discuss a scraper, a tool with which on Saturday
mornings I had a love-hate relationship. Love equalled
spending money. Hate stood for the pong from
dropping boards in hen huts which occasionally I
helped to scrape. Roman coins had been found at the
foot of the hill and Matey speculated whether a Roman

scraper had been unearthed showing continuity with boys of the past.

Hens, pullets, chickens ran into scores and into each other sometimes. All except one cabinful at a later time were free range but at dusk Dad toured his little empire with a storm lamp to shut down the hen-sized bob-holes against a fox. I never saw a fox and perhaps Dad didn't but with unnatural lack of faith he seemed to expect one. Most of our hen cabins were lined up like Boy Scouts. Others were tucked into hollows in the top pasture, which may have been defence, or coal outcrop ditches. Night soil apart, I got on well with the hens. We had some sort of kinship. I was a free range boy allowed to stray around the farm except after dark, coming in only for the "corn".

Hens varied in temperament and gave little performances. They would cluck like plucked guitars and after laying go for the high notes like some opera diva. Mother hens like theatre shrews would scatter dogs or cats to protect their chicks. Cockerels, plump and sometimes camp, would challenge rival males. As for melodramas, you looked no further than old "broilers" which would flap around, and take longer to expire than a Shakespearean ham. Alas, alack, the invention of battery houses would close down the outdoor theatre of the free range thespians.

Poultry farming had its tricks of the trade. Pot eggs in boxes encouraged laying. Shell grit was fed to prevent eggs arriving with soft shells. Rhode Island Reds were seen as reliable layers. Dad hatched some chickens in incubators, the soft warm glow giving a cosy feeling in the outbuilding. We looked each year for the wet and break-through chicks. A less pleasing operation was the creosoting of hen huts for protection. At least Dad was spared the fate of a seventeenth-century local Quaker whose henhouse was demolished and one hen taken for refusing tithes.

It was eggs in and with everything. Our nightmares ought to have been oval. Eggs boiled. Eggs fried. Eggs poached. Eggs scrambled. Eggs in baskets, buckets, boxes and theatre. In rare spare moments, breaking off for a smoke perhaps, Dad would entertain with bucket circus. The bucket was his prop and he would fill it with water and then swing it in an arc over his head. Not a drop left the bucket. Our eyes widened even more as he took up a bucket half filled with unwashed eggs. Surely, it would become the biggest omelette on record, with Mother spared the job of washing one batch of eggs at least. "Ladies and gentlemen . . .". Up and over went the farmer's lean and muscled arm into swift half circuits of fresh air. The price of eggs had never been so high. Yet not a hairline fracture showed on any shell and his act taught us more about gravity than a physics lesson. "Do you dare me," I would say as I tried the act with minimal water and got a pint-sized shower the first time. I was not allowed to send eggs into orbit.

Sadly, farms are not all circuses and hayrides and play fights with dogs. That would be Paradise which we understood would come much later if we were good. There was another, gloomier side. Even on days when the sun dried mown grass and allowed us to play-focus its rays through magnifying glass to burn paper, shadows would be slanting across the yard. As a thespian cockerel might have crowed "parting is such sweet sorrow". For the partings were the worst. They sometimes signalled *death*. The living I loved. The culling I loathed. But killing has to be the last act in some farming and before the end of the plot I'd slip out of the audience as Mother conspired for someone's Sunday dinner and Dad might murmur, "he'll never make a farmer". I'd seen hens scatter like a burst water main when one was grabbed for "black cap" sentencing. I was sure it knew its hour had come. The twist, crack, feather dance of death were not for me. "It's only a reflex action" never reassured me. Because of other demands Dad left most of the dispatching to Mother who would do it as humanely as she could. There would be no pleasure in it. Farmers got attached to their animals, talked to them, especially on small intimate farms. Townspeople collecting cowpat souvenirs on pumps and other unsuitable walking shoes could hear more than the terse commands to working dog or horse. Our cattle were called in with a "cowp cowp cowp" call, and our hens with a clucking sound, mocking them almost. Who knows what went on in the minds of such creatures, and what they made of us, the two-legged animals and our right to command.

Nature's killers did not practise our calculated humanity. A bird of prey would cleanse small life from sight by hovering, an instinctive butcher whose methods we might condemn while accepting his role in the control of vermin. My mercy in saving a mouse from a playful cat would not be shown by marauding birds, including the owl which shared his night with bats and moths, the latter inclined to approach lamplight through windows and flutter off with a headache muttering "never saw that".

So, the sentencing of hens and even mice was a torment to a sensitive boy, but that of the goose was another, and bigger. Sometimes we would acquire a moving object that was out of character for us. Perhaps friends taking a holiday would say "can you look after this for us" and never take "this" back. By some osmosis the goose arrived. All went smoothly enough. She was fed and watered and chatted to and blended in with animals, hens and humans and never dashed, cackling and spitting, towards strangers, as some watchgeese do. She managed to avoid the Dewhurst baptismal, perhaps wisely for she would probably have been saddled with Mother Goose. One day without warning the Goose Reaper arrived and I happened on the hapless chapel pair contemplating goosecide with a yard brush on the creature's neck. As remembered, she was spared, but the recollection used to make me shiver as if she'd walked over my grave.

They were the gentlest, my parents. Sticks were held out to steer cattle and not to hurt them. Frail chicks were nursed to health and sick animals cosseted. But some actions on a farm call for some pain. Surplus kittens had to be drowned, usually in tears, piglets eased out of sows, horses driven on bits. Pigs squealed almost without handling and when the tumbril came Matey would be upstairs, head under pillow. I believed animals could smell their fate and as we had so few it was like parting with friends on death or departure to fresh fields. Rosycheeks was not just another cow, number six in the shippon, a prying head over a wall, one of a committee on a hilltop in fine weather. She was, well, Rosycheeks, and mourned as named and known and cared for. Hens were too numerous to name or know but customers on the milk round could be sure of fresh eggs from hens which had the freedom of the farm by the hill.

CHAPTER
NINE

Black, Blacker, Blackest

The remedy is worse than the disease.
Francis Bacon

Mother and maternal grandmother between them had remedies for every ailment in the medical dictionary except, perhaps, a cracked skull, and if I'd offered them that challenge they would have hunted for something to slap on it, sniff up or consume. "Tek it. It'll do you good." Often the doing of good seemed worse than the problem. Commonest were toothache and earache. Toothache called for a hot damp cloth sprinkled with pepper or, if they had it in, Sloan's liniment applied to the cheek and which smelled more like a lotion for horses. It literally outsmarted the pain. Loosen a tooth and dad would practise his skills as an engineer by engineering a piece of thread from tooth to oven door-knob. "It'll not tek a second. You'll not feel it." The door slammed. The tooth was out. The truth was out. I felt it. Earache required the heart of a boiled onion to be smuggled into the ear, leaving the outer layers for the pan. Mother wasted nothing. I never knew whether some other mothers asked the greengrocer

57

for a pound of onions "in case our lad gets earache, you know".

Several prospects for time off school came with the proclamation: "He's got a rash." Chicken pox, scarlet fever, measles and its European cousin German measles mottled children's skins. Mumps sounded funny but wasn't and certainly not worth missing algebra for. Sick people were said to be "under't doctor" and if such a gentleman was making a house call there would be a flurry of tidying up and bed changing to "get straight". The stethoscope was an expected authority and only much later would we hear of an old Welsh farmer who insisted on its use. The house-call doctor who'd forgotten it achieved some satisfaction by listening through his foot pump to the old man's chest.

Goose grease, Germolene, Zam-Buk and Belladonna could have been from the chapel pantomime. They were from the medicine cupboard. Iodine stung like the cane. Dock leaves soothed nettle stings but seemed scarce around nettles. Camomile calmed sunburn. Compo warmed. Black treacle was "to make you go". A sweaty sock with some pungent addition helped a sore throat. A hot-water bottle in its knitted jacket settled stomach-ache. Or so they claimed. More earthy was Dad's alleged cure for warts — the rinsing of the offender with urine or, more precisely, "maiden's water". My family conspired to make doctors redundant. Colds were common and my cycling Aunt Florrie claimed to take hers to the top of Pinhaw, a Yorkshire moor, and leave it there. I'd little faith in

Pinhaw as a tip for the deposit of nose candles but I once lanced a boil on a playground slide in Yorkshire.

Worse, perhaps, was being closeted in the bedroom with ghosts and goblins. For a chesty complaint Mother would light a small oil lamp with overhead tray, black from use. The cure, a pungent liquid called Cresoline, dispersed a vapour for inhaling which cast shadows on ceiling and walls, a haunting version of the finger shadowgraph for making birds and animals. It was "for your own good" but for a boy who required the stairs door open against imagined fears it was a nightmare. Nightmare was a strange word. Were children who took naps in daylight pestered by a daymare? Bedtime readings helped us to sleep though some might have had a nightmare from too much obsession with the baby who crashed down from a broken bough or our male misfortune to be made from frogs, snails and puppy dogs' tails. Perhaps some children were unwisely offered the bedtime executioners, "Here comes a candle to light you to bed, Here comes a chopper to chop off your head." Our "Gentle Jesus meek and mild" bedside prayer had at least the promise of a restful night.

Blackest of all were the funerals, though as children we were usually spared the bleakness of the day itself. Funerals were for adults, drawn together like rooks in head-to-toe black. The gloom could be suffocating and no boy would want to be part of it from choice. After the laying out and the undertaker's "offices" the lying-in-state in terraced houses was in the front parlours where the coffin had pride of place.

Neighbours arranged house-to-house collections for wreaths, curtains were drawn and callers encouraged to pay last respects to the loved one in the light available. As the veil was drawn back a consoler would fumble for some suitable word. "Looks just like him, doesn't it!" It never did from my limited inclusion in the ritual. Almost more depressing than the gloom was the smell of death that lingered, heavily scented flowers and the stale odour of decay, long revived by a whiff of the white flowers of hawthorn in May. Much later I would learn that the may flower contains the same chemical that occurs in decaying tissue.

On funeral day the minister allowed himself a brief smile at the house before the practised monotone. Respect for the dead was total. Neighbours' curtains closed without question and as the cortége inched towards churchyard or cemetery hats came off men's heads as if triggered by a device on the hearse, as certain as a man touching his hat to a lady or offering her his seat on a bus. Black shoes only. Black, blacker, blackest, as underlined in Stanley Holloway's monologue about Jim who'd given his black boots to someone with none, and wore brown boots for a funeral.

Mourners retired afterwards for a meal based around ham in home or local café. Rain, never scarce in Lancashire, added to the dejection, and film directors hoping for a shiver to open some atmospheric thriller looked no further than mourners and umbrellas, black of course, edged like the borders of a funeral card around a grave. Some youths passed into manhood shouldering the coffins of close relatives, a metaphor almost for the belief that they were then able to shoulder responsibility. Small coffins were the chillest sight, the harrowing farewells to a boy or girl taken by one of the killers of the time, like the dreaded diphtheria.

CHAPTER
TEN

The Milky Way

And milk comes frozen home in pail.
William Shakespeare

Dad's blue milk van had curved mudguards, sidelights like halves of eggs boiled hard and black, and round windows in the sides. It lived in non-delivery hours in a stone outbuilding opposite the farmhouse. A horse-drawn float with ornate lamps and a jalopy with running boards and overhead sales slogan had gone before in the service of customers. I remembered little of those, the blue van coinciding with my awareness, though some farmers were still loyal to the horse, clattering with their Dollys and Sams and rattling cans on their spoked wheels, wrapped against the Pennine winds and rain in the stone town, and its council housing estates.

The blue van seemed cramped for three big milk kits (some called them churns), assorted cans in gill, pint and quart sizes, egg boxes, a milkgirl aunt and, when possible, a Matey milkboy crouched in the back ready to deliver from the back step. We would leave the farm with our own boxed eggs but with clean empty kits to be filled with fresh morning milk at the end of the lane where dad bought it from Marsden Hall Farm above the old hall of the same name. It was in Marsden in the seventeenth century that Ambrose Walton of the hall was arrested as one of the leaders of a riot believed to be against a Sunday observance decree to the "displeasure of God". No such displeasuring occurred during Dad's calls, though there was one minor incident. I was on the back step thinking of anything but algebra when Dad pushed one of the big kits towards me. My mouth argued with its lid and the bottom was chipped off two teeth. They were probably milk teeth and the encounter would have been dismissed by Ambrose and his rowdy men as small beer.

Nelson was a stone maze to me but dad knew it with the knowledge a milkman acquires. "I've been in every street in Nelson," he told me, and was admired for such thoroughness until I found that one of its streets was called Every. Even on my limited outings on the back step I got some purchase on the town's geography as we served the close-knit terraces that marched up and down cobbled gaslit streets with their corner shops, chippies, mills, chapels and working men's clubs, more clubs than public houses. It was said that Burnley had more pubs in its main street than Nelson's entire number. If that came from Dad, a non-drinker, it would be hearsay rather than experience, though he might expect it to increase milk consumption.

On working days weavers who had jobs were already mee-mawing across the racket of looms as the van delivered and in hot weather, with weaving shed doors open, the sound bombarded the streets. Mills were known by names of their owners, Jimmy Nelson's, Sam Holden's (Barrowford) and others. The van zig-zagged past workers' homes with steps mopped and donkey-stoned and edged with white, and Dad said some of them were "little palaces" inside. Many customers went to church or chapel and were neighbours in the biblical sense, helping each other, borrowing cupfuls of sugar, swapping recipes, minding each others' children. Doors were left unlocked while housewives slipped to the corner shop. Trust was endemic.

As Dad ladled milk from kit to can I'd dash to doorsteps or window sills to supply everything from jugs to jam jars, topped with saucers against dust or cat. Dad would cruise to the next call. "The horse used to know its round", he'd say, "and move on to the next customer on its own." Could it have been one of his customers who also presented her jug to the "selling out shop" for beer for her husband? Once, she fell over and smashed the jug on the pavement. "Hard luck that," the doctor said, attending to her minor injury. "Could have bin worse," she said. "Could hev bin coming back wi' t' jug full."

Washing was dried and carpets aired in the back streets. One woman who put a carpet over a dustbin to air off found two neighbours about to make off with it, and share half each: "We thowt it were for't dustbin chap." Mondays were traditional washing days and back streets would be strung with its bunting. Only a masochist milkman, coalman or rag o' bone man would gatecrash a washing line after all the possing, boiling, dolly blueing, rinsing and mangling that had gone on.

Sometimes a housewife would want an extra pint or two without warning. "Our Alice and kids are coming." If too many Alices turned up unexpectedly a milkman could run out of milk and be helped out by another. Dad knew most of those who served the town by their name and farm. "That's Cannon," he'd say. Or Crowther. Or Begley. "That's Joe Errington from Slitterforth up behind us." I used to think Slitterforth was a strange name. Cannon was from Shelfield Farm which could only have been a coincidence. Although it was smart to spot potential customers "flitting" into an empty house there seemed to be as much warmth as rivalry among milkmen.

Mill chimneys sent soiled grey mufflers to the sky. The van pottered past the homes of clothlookers, weavers, twisters and drawers, warp dressers, unemployed workers and the "Manchester men" of cotton who took morning trains to the Cotton Exchange. Perhaps they were the ones with gardens and leaded windows. Unions and clubs echoed the jobs. Overlookers serviced looms and generated tacklers' tales along the following lines:

"Is he in, luv?"
"No. Haven't you heard? He died last week."
"Oh, I'm sorry, luv. Did he say owt about a tin o' paint?"
Man hurrying for a train, misses it.
"As ter missed it?" asked a mate.

"Nay, I didn't like look on it so I chased it out o't'station."

Buses had appeared three years before me but trams carried on till 1934 when the mayor stayed up until midnight to travel on the last one. In his milk-rounding Dad had been trundling past scissors grinders, muffin men with basketed heads and sometimes a wooden leg, epilogue to the Great War. He passed chimney fires and sweeps' brushes thrust like shocked heads out of chimneys. He passed: Frederick Scott FBOA, optician with his "qualified refractionists"; Victory V gums and lozenges for cold journeys: "Don't disturb the service"; Haworth's, spruce black beer (1d on empty bottles); Hartley's chemists: Jessop's Linctus, "Keep our winter cold at bay"; Spencers' brides' cakes of distinction; Blakey Ranges Ltd, "thoroughly seasoned timber"; Chappell and Son, "We tailor on the premises".

Breathless fire engines clanged past him. It was the night I'd been encouraged from bed to window to witness a night sky lit by a blaze which was to gut the town's market hall and public clock. A boy gave the alarm and as local firemen fought the impossible a fire pump from Colne broke its driving chain at a top dash of 15 miles an hour. Iced hoses hampered pumping from the canal. The faithful clock, which had been chiming the hour for twenty-six years, offered 10p.m. in its last gasp and expired. Its minute hand hung down, motionless. A temporary market hall would eventually replace it and sell us hot black peas. Elsewhere you could call for a Foulds's blood tonic drink, start up jingly behind-shop-door-bells and watch your purchase money spirited away on an aerial system. The smell of newly baked bread was a treat but I could never gaze into the butcher's raw red display. Toys or cycles on sale would stop me dead but none compared with toffee shops and their bottled glories — aniseed balls, sarsaparilla tablets, coconut mushrooms, Spanish braid, kali and other fillips to the dental profession. "You'll suffer. You'll have no teeth left." I did and I haven't but squandering them was the icing on a childhood.

Town was noisy. Town was tiring. Town was tight with smells and sounds and sights. On lighter nights children improvised back street "theatre". Clothes-maidens and blankets became schools, hospital wards, Sunday Schools. "I'll be teacher. You were it yesterday." Jerseys were goalposts. Wickets were chalked on the back of lavatory and coalplace walls. Money was scarce and imagination flourished. Girls balanced on mothers' high heels, skipped, played hopscotch and in May, the merry, merry month of, danced around maypoles made from broom-handles and coloured paper. Her Majesty perched on a kitchen buffet or a box and dreamed she was the Queen of England. Boys played marbles with dull browns and more distinguished glassies, hot through with colours. They strung conkers, made guys, stuck to gas tar, dared this and that and spit and belched to mark their difference. Both sexes whipped tops and played hide and seek. "123456789ten. Comingreadyornot."

Some milk lads left school at fourteen and became full-timers. Some were farmers' sons giving a hand to subsidise the comic market. Boys' work was spied on by School Board men, known to some as "kid hunters". Dad was no law-breaker but once I had my head pushed gently down out of School Board sight when one of these predators closed in. Perhaps it was in school hours and I was improving from some illness and being removed from "around your mother's feet". Another predator, a public health official, would officially swoop without warning to take samples of milk from the van for testing. Officially.

Milk bills were often settled in kitchens. Front parlours were for the weekend, especially wet weekends, when dads made flaming sorties from kitchen to front room with half of the kitchen fire on a fire shovel, threatening carpet, house, if not life itself. Many a *Daily Herald* caught fire drawing a sulking fire into life. When it seemed circumspect, and not before, courting couples were allowed an hour's cuddling under the oily eye of the *Monarch of the Glen* with curtains closed against prying gas lamp and that nosy woman across the street.

Town had its characters but the best known lived on only in the minds of my elders from early in the century. Dummy was one, a deaf and dumb man who haunted the streets. He was, they reminisced, dressed in poor clothing and harmless enough, gave a thumbs-up greeting and smile, but, less happily, attracted the teasing of children. Jimmy Trodge, a farmer's son from Lomeshaye, was apparently employed as a drover of cattle to and from farms to Nelson station for Skipton auction mart. It was said that Rupert Whittaker, manager of the DeLuxe cinema in Railway Street, used to let Jimmy in free and treat him to an ice-cream.

John and Jane were a tiny pair from Wheatley Lane above the town, known to some as "Worsthorne Johnny and his little shuffling wife". John, in bowler hat and beard, had been a farmhand and according to which handed-down intelligence you believed had peddled blacking for clogs, hawked clothes pegs, or sold cinders from a donkey and cart, with Jane loading the cinder bag on to his back. They were reported to adjourn each evening to a village public house to fill a gallon stone bottle with beer and after imbibing settle down to sleep on the hearth rather than in bed.

Apart from "bad payers" Dad had good relations with his customers, with blessed spin-offs for Matey — vanilla slices, surplus, from a bakery and a box of Meccano parts from a "better-off" family whose son had outgrown them. The Victory V works, the town centre clock and the Destructor, which sounded like a horror film monster and devoured the town's rubbish, were landmarks on the milk round. Dad supplied eggs to a cheese stall on the open market with its noseful of aromas. Sometimes, on the way home, we'd buy oatcakes to eat with butter and golden syrup or dry over the clothes rack to harden and eat with stew.

Milk vans might not always start on damp mornings, but given careful parking, wouldn't run away. Not so one milk horse which took off up Railway Street with its float swaying behind and with an unexpected delivery of milk and scrambled eggs across the street. The float was damaged, the horse only slightly hurt. It was, by coincidence, April Fool's day. The town looked for its milk whatever the weather and milkmen obliged through fog, snow and ice. The ghostly clanking of chains on van wheels and the tap of clogs against walls to knock off snow pads were sometimes the only early morning music on muffled streets. Blown snow used to drift into our one-sided lane and at times, not often, the van had to be dug out from the farm, and once part of a wall demolished to allow a detour. Dad wore two coats in wretched weather and some milkmen in open floats would throw an old sack over their shoulders. Cotton benefited from a damp climate but milkmen under cats-and-dogs rain would wish it far enough.

Once, and only briefly, perhaps obliging a friend, we kept a cow that had to be milked. Even the squeezing of milk from a teat was an acquired art and Mother had mastered it and in milking would squirt the occasional warm mouthful towards me. Cow hands used to turn the knebs of their caps back to front for milking and much later I heard of one gullible soul who was persuaded by a leg-puller that the caps were bought like that and went off to the market to look for a cap with a kneb at the back. Who knows, perhaps they sold him one in Yorkshire.

CHAPTER
ELEVEN

Bread & Water Magic

One day, while farmers and milkmen were out delivering milk, word came from the shadow of Pendle Hill of an unusual experiment to try to find one of their number who'd been missing from home. The experimenters arrived on the banks of Ogden Reservoir with a loaf of bread, not for their elevenses but for a search of its waters.

Relatives of an elderly farmer believed that he might have fallen into the reservoir and they'd already asked the Corporation if its water could be run off. As no clothing or the man's walking stick had been found nearby the authorities declined, and so it was that what the local newspaper called "black magic" was being attempted in the haunts of the alleged witches of local history. The water had been dragged once without success. The experimenters placed quicksilver inside the loaf which was then floated on the reservoir, the theory being that it would float to rest over the place where a body was lying.

The experiment failed. A Pendleside breeze was blamed for blowing the loaf off course. A second attempt also came to nothing, a clear case of casting your bread on the waters without return and no doubt local farmers had some choice and head-scratching comments on the affair, speculating perhaps whether "them from't town had been using their loaf". The farmer, sadly, was later found drowned but not by means of the floating bread.

Life had its tragic and lighter moments. Bread and circuses apart, the old haunt of the witch shenanigans got itself a somewhat curious pride in its Pendle Forest Balloon Juice Company which on the evening of 29 April 1935 met for what it called its Royal Jubilee observance. A Signor Martini presided over a "distinguished" gathering where one of the representatives argued that Twiston, more hamlet than village, should be given one of the latest aero-fire engines by monthly instalments and with an assurance that it would be delivered by "plain van". Flight Admiral "Flashpast" Johnson said Twiston's only resource for outbreaks was an old hansom cab equipped with garden squirts. The agreement should carry the condition that two farmers and a plumber (registered) should sign as guarantors and then Twiston could have this as a feature of the Royal Jubilee celebrations.

We, on our side of the valley, never discovered whether a "plain van" was sent for members of the meeting but certainly those who called for balloon juice from the company, invented by a local licensee, would be the same who later sought supplies from the Trawden and Sabden treacle mines in the area and the products of the parkin weavers and, who knows, in years to come their descendants probably went on to shop at the Ken Dodd jam butty mines.

CHAPTER
TWELVE

The Phantom Painter

Small town, great renown.
François Rabelais

Not much happened by the hill, nothing much to startle the horse or scatter the hens. They used to say there were "nowt as funny as folk" and as more than 30,000 "folk" lived in town it didn't take the class genius to work out that most funny things, that is funny to laugh at or funny peculiar, would happen there. Most of such reports came second or third hand from milk round, school or Sunday School and from occasional contact with two sources in the upper town, the chip shop and the clogger's. Some boys could add barber's to that but I was usually parted from surplus hair by the family scissors though, thankfully, not finished off like an upside-down pudding basin to be marked out for the jibe "he's had bowl on 'is 'ead".

With time I'd be dispatched to the nearest of Nelson's shoal of fish and chip shops for a bicycle take-away, down the lane, over a hump of ash emulating Robbie, the trick rider, past the Open Air School and looking for a quick return before fish and chips in yesterday's *Daily Herald* got cold. The clogger's was near my junior school and held more prospect for news because the stay was longer and the clientèle warm, seated and gossipy. I seemed to spend half a childhood watching the clogger, tacks in teeth, hunched over repairs in his iron and alder cell to give a bright new spark on iron against pavements. We marvelled that he never swallowed a tack as we sat in stockinged feet, wondering if some school bully would be humbled by sparkless rubber treads.

It may have been from some clogger's, barber's or milk round that the town had got wind of the phantom painter in a whispering breeze that had gathered force and blew round town: "Hey, has ter sin yon steps at town 'all?" The head cleaner, reporting for work on a Monday morning in 1935, had got an eyeful first. It was more eyesore than eyecatching. The main entrance steps to the town hall had been painted red, white and blue and a side wall enamelled with lines in the same colours. "God Save the King" was emblazoned on a panel. Whatever else, the phantom painter, or painters, sneaking with tins and brushes through the cobbled streets at dead of night was for king and country or trouble-making, or all three.

To us boys the phantom would be of more interest than the politics of the time but from the wireless and no doubt from school we would know this was Silver Jubilee year for King George and Queen Mary, and His Majesty had gleamed from a classy magazine in naval uniform, all smothered in gold braid. Only with time would we understand that the town's Socialist council was concerned for free school dinners, unemployment and other pressing needs and had kept back shillings which the County Council wished to be spent on the young. The local council's token gesture had been a Union Jack on its flagpole until the overnight dauber had finished his work of art. Whether I was among many oglers of the stepscape I couldn't recall but perhaps Dad on his round would see it all, and the painted mayoral lamp too, before the erasers wiped out the memory and any jeers and anger on either side had subsided. What we had flying at the farm, if anything, was forgotten but apparently the town itself, town hall apart, had celebrations, rosettes, flags and church bells in what the *Nelson Leader* called an "extraordinary display" of public loyalty.

As the Jubilee beacons on hills and the chalked slogans, "We want our bobs", began to fade towards history we were pen-and-inking our way in junior school towards a new secondary setting for our education. Nelson's relatively brief history and politics were for the specialists in each, but with time I would learn that its council had reforming policies for its people, a nonconforming approach to some issues and, for some, a pacific vein. The local Member of Parliament, Sydney Silverman, was himself a peace advocate and spirited campaigner for the abolition of capital punishment, and in the June to come in 1936 an uncommon murder would darken the town with a grim sequel at Strangeways Prison in Manchester, which would again focus minds on the hanging debate.

CHAPTER
THIRTEEN

The Unquiet Tuesday

Murder wol out; certain it wol not faille.
Geoffrey Chaucer

Shopkeepers in Nelson took their half-day break on Tuesdays. Blinds came down and doors closed and gave the town centre an orphaned look. Anyone going there for goods or gossip after dinner-time on that day would be disappointed. The trails had gone cold on any tittle-tattle that had mouthed its way through shops in the morning. But on one Tuesday in June 1936, my last full year at junior school, there was a frisson known usually to readers of Agatha Christie. By evening the stark round robin of a bizarre double murder had flown through mills and offices and sullied the headlines of the evening newspaper.

It had happened in Clayton Street, next to the very Every Street which Dad joked about and on his morning round in that area of town was sending a chill through the summer. Some of his customers knew personally and others by sight the elderly woman, perhaps around Miss Marple's age, whose death had sent the Chief Constable and a squad of officers across Lancashire to investigate the first murder of its kind in the town for nearly forty years. A quiet Tuesday? Not for them.

As the mills thundered away a Home Office pathologist was conducting a post-mortem not only on Miss Ruth Clarkson, aged seventy-four, but also on her pet dog Roy, a wire-haired fox terrier and inseparable companion in life and death. A deeply religious and somewhat eccentric spinster, Miss Clarkson lived alone with Roy, often seen padding beside her on shopping visits to the town centre. As she hadn't been seen for several days policemen broke in and found her with multiple head wounds. The dog was hanging from a bedpost. Miss Clarkson had goods and jewellery from a former unmarried companion. She had neglected herself and was described variously as well educated, charming and reserved, and had been expected at an evangelical meeting on the Monday night.

Max Mayer Haslam, who was twenty-three and an unemployed cotton spinner, was found guilty of the murder. He was only 4ft 7ins in height and was said to look "pathetically childlike" between policemen at the committal hearing. At Manchester Assizes, where he was sentenced to death, he maintained his innocence, claiming the woman and dog were dead before he broke in to rob her. Miss Clarkson's funeral was held in secret. She was buried in the vault of her former woman companion.

Such harrowing, if rare, deeds were discussed by adults in whispers, or out of our hearing, not least the chilling sequel on a grey February day in 1937, by coincidence my eleventh birthday, when the last act in the tragedy was the hanging of Haslam at the forbidding Strangeways Prison in Manchester. Campaigners in a serial crusade against capital punishment were outside the gaol in protest. As the *Nelson Leader*, our mirror on events grim or gay, put it:

> On the stroke of nine a voice from a loudspeaker invited the men present to remove their hats. The hymn "Abide with Me" was relayed and then out of the unseen the voice declaimed "another state murder has been committed. Another insane man has been sent into eternity." The hymn "Nearer my God to Thee" rose balefully from the subdued voices and so ended the demonstrations. At 9.15am notices were hung on the prison door announcing that the execution of Haslam had taken place.

The same day some Nelsoners were enjoying *The Trail of the Lonesome Pine*, a romance in the Kentucky Hills, at the Deluxe picture house. Down the road in Burnley some of its people were at a variety show *Sit Back and Laugh* (twice nightly, twice brightly). Life went on.

One of the personalities in the Clarkson case was Mr E.G. Robey, prosecuting, a nephew of George Robey, the comedian. Another, Chief Inspector Green, had had charge of the Ruxton murders in Lancaster the previous year of Dr Buck Ruxton's wife Isabella and their nursemaid Mary Jane Rogerson for which the doctor was executed. Parts of a dismembered body were found in a river north of Moffatt in Scotland and the case was noted for achievements in forensic pathology. It produced a melodramatic children's song:

Red stains on the carpet, red stains on the knife
For Dr Buck Ruxton has murdered his wife.
The maidservant saw it and threatened to tell
So Dr Buck Ruxton, he's killed her as well.

The bleak lines would be parroted in northern school yards, possibly in our own, with the flippant innocence of childhood. Mercifully such acts, though grist to the adult gossip mill, were rare. How long the squalid affair of Miss Clarkson and Roy would be remembered was uncertain but the Ruxton murders would echo through the years with the doctor's home in its square in Lancaster being the object of morbid curiosity. The abolitionists had demonstrated at both executions but with the Haslam hanging there would be more interest locally, especially because of the campaign of Sydney Silverman to put men like Albert Pierrepoint, the public hangman, out of office. Pierrepoint was in a direct line from Richard Brandon who executed Charles I and from John Ketch, known as Jack, who became caricatured for the "delight" of children in the Punch and Judy show.

No such fate as that of Charles was waiting for our new sovereign, George VI, and in my last year at Junior School, in Mr Eastwood's class, we celebrated the new king's coronation. Nelson was now described as one of the "best-decorated" towns in north-east Lancashire. It was 1937, the year in which the German ambassador gave the new king a Nazi salute, and our market hall, mills, streets and, yes, the town hall too, were flagged and buntinged and I was among 3,800 children shrieking on to playing fields for sports, tea and presentation souvenirs, though I don't know who counted us all. Coronation mugs were on offer but perhaps my most vivid image of that day was of a carthorse on the field that broke its leg and had, in the cleansing jargon, to be "put down", a poignant wrench for a farmer's son.

So we had a new king and queen but by then northern towns had had a queen or two of their own. From a cotton industry that had suffered from disabling foreign competition and other problems the cotton queen had emerged to weave a thread or two of colour into the lives of the mill workers. Mill girls could be wrenched from loom to crown. Various titles appeared and in the mid-thirties, for example, Miss Joyce Horne, silk examiner at Clover Mill, had found herself chosen as "Most Beautiful Mill Girl" from a thousand photographs and nine finalists at the Bolton Palais de Dance to take the silver rose-bowl. We wouldn't remember where Joyce and her beauty and other bowl winners would officiate but before and into the early part of the war to come the town was host to Ideal Homes exhibitions, Sanger's Circus, the Hallé Orchestra, Flotsam and Jetsam, entertainers, Jack Payne and Henry Hall, band leaders, Cossack horsemen, Jimmy Maxton MP and Oswald Mosley, fascist. Perhaps echoes of, and the need for, a clog dance held in the mid-thirties for a clog fund, were fading.

With the coronation behind us, and them, their Majesties were to call on us in the year to come, my first full year at secondary school. The family album would acquire a snap of Matey in a loyal flush of secondary school caps among 4.000 children waiting in Carr Road for the royal pair. Some caps, including mine, looked older than first-year secondary, as if footballed around the school cloakroom. Caps, rakish, scruffy, new and named or not, must have been appreciated, for their Majesties were to express "especial delight" at seeing so many children under them, most waving flags or emblems. So reported the *Nelson Leader*, though in our photograph there was only one flag stick to be seen and its owner was sucking it. After the king and queen had left their official dais women hurried up to sit in the chair which Her Majesty had occupied against the loyal blue and white gloxinias and bright red carnations — prompting, one could imagine, one or two domestic exchanges over the tea table that afternoon.

"Hey Jack, you'll never guess what I've bin up to this afternoon. I've sat down where t'queen sat on her own private chair on that platform thing, daisy or summat they calls it. Mind you, I wasn't first up them steps. That Mrs Thingamy from no. 8, you know wi t'gammy legs, fair ran up them steps, gammy legs an' all, to plonk down first. I bet chair were still warm. It were that lovely sat there, Jack, flowers an' all that. Would you like to have done it?"

"I wouldn't, Maggie. What wants to sit on't queen's seat, warm or not? They're only like you and me, yer know. Ready for a sit down. There's nowt clever about it."

CHAPTER
FOURTEEN

A Schooling

"We call him tortoise because he taught us;" said the Mock Turtle angrily. "Really you are very dull."

Lewis Carroll

So it was to be a new school, and a walk down the fields to it. In the spring of my last half-year at St John's a thousand children from local schools had steamed off in charter trains to Edinburgh in what was officially termed an "educational tour" but some would see as temporary relief from arithmetic. We saw the castle, Forth Bridge and other sights, and heard the city's one o'clock gun and probably told the Scots that we had a ten o'clock town hooter. Alderman Andrew Smith, Education Committee chairman, reporting back, said there had been no accident of "any moment".

One little boy had been pecked at by a duck at the zoo but soon recovered. It wasn't me who tried to take it home, sir!

After junior school the road to education forked. Farmers, with all parents, speculated about what was on offer and the "lottery" to achieve it. Some farmers looked to their sons to inherit their cockerel dawns, fresh air with essence of pigsty, weather roulette and, for some, "nowt much in't bank to show for it". For others the grass beyond was greener. "Ged a good schooling, lad. Don't be knee-deep in cow muck all thi life. Ged a good 'ead on thi." Dad had given nothing except his body language away. He wasn't of the soil himself and his shrugs mimed acceptance that I could never harm a flea on a cat. Delighted by set — landscapes tied in time, muslin dawns, snow sculptures, bronze autumns, rainbows and, once, the northern lights — the understudy preferred book or cycle ride to back end of cow and could never take the lead. Dad understood and one day when he arrived home with six encyclopedias with mauve covers and knowledge from A to Z I knew it. We approached that fork in the road at eleven with some dread and lost good friends by the narrowest of examination margins and, probably, from test nerves on examination day.

Nelson Secondary School for Boys and Girls was, like the farm, on the town boundary with Colne, between the railway and the public cemetery. It was already developing some reputation for academic progress and sport though had scant prospect of Matey enhancing either. It was the year in which King George VI was crowned, his abdicated brother married Wallis Simpson and the notorious rector of Stiffkey was mauled by a lion at Skegness. The matriarchs in my family kept a loyal scrutiny on the doings of the royals and the love story that cost us the ruler of an empire on which the sun never set. Most of these bulletins by Leslie Mitchell and others from the box with knobs for twiddling on the dresser, adult matters, were of minor concern to a boy, though I'd perk up at the item on the lion and rector. Lion mauling was uncommon and of more interest than kingdoms.

As I trembled into my new school that September, green with yellow badges and, camouflaged among others, I was probably more concerned about who I would sit next to, which House I would hinder and whether the stop-me-and-buy-one tricycle would be outside with its penny Snofrutes as promised. (Should that be who or whom I would sit next to, Miss Welch?) The headmaster was George Mutch, former pupil and physics master at the school, a cricketer and with an MC from the Great War. He was a gentle man, determined if required, but apart from slowing me down once or twice on corridors I wouldn't have to approach him, which meant I was neither genius nor scallywag but someone somewhere in between. It almost seemed that most teachers would welcome a feeble nickname to none at all, making them at least seem noticed. We were soon talking Swisher, Dubbin, Weedy, Bulldog, Henneck, among others. I was immersed into B stream, a sort of second division form, and recruited to hamper Thursby House, colour red matching the hair. Boys quickly found they had left their first names behind. While girls continued as Marion, Dorothy or Jean we became Dewhurst, Hartley, Leedham, which seemed like a sanction in itself though less so than "that boy" or "you boy" which varied the form of address. My form would include a

King, Fox, Burgess, Fryer (boys) and a Fortune and a Precious (girls).

The school was teaching under the shadows of recession and ultimately of war and we were to lose masters to military service and welcome evacuees. We would see our *Torch* magazine list former students on war service, some never to return home — an MC for a captain, the death of a trooper in North Africa, a sailor imprisoned by the Japanese and many more.

By then we'd decided on our likes and dislikes on the school timetable. No chemistry developed between me and that subject. It had nothing to do with smells, for even hydrogen sulphide couldn't compete with some on the farm. Mr Chambers, a chemistry master, was the only teacher that I persuaded to sign my autograph album, perhaps while he was waiting for something to change colour, but even that didn't win me over. Boiling and bubbling like some dark rite from the Pendle witches the chemi lab never put its spell on me and I swapped litmus papers for Latin, a dead language to which Miss Jump gave a spirited jump start. Nothing around her could die or doze. Latin was paired with biology in the swap for which my walk to school via birds and botany gave a little preparation.

Mathematics employed a succession of masters whose surname also began with the letter M — Myers, Mulligan, MacDonald — any one of whom could probably work out the mathematical probability of that coincidence. Two Ms and a Mr Williams laboured to interest us in Pythagoras and co. and a mystic maze called algebra which had letters for numbers in a non-English subject. In years to come I would empathise with J.M. Barrie's question: "What is algebra exactly? Is it those three-cornered things?" One master was a considerable marksman with the chalk missiles and together with a boy who ate it for a bet must have cost the Borough a penny rate in chalk. As for the chalk thrower, he was reported to have fallen asleep next to a boy on a bus journey to Manchester, dropped off in mid-sentence and wakened up to finish the sentence.

From reports on my efforts with protractor and ruler on those algebraic conundrums I must have accounted, at a conservative estimate, for 10 per cent of the grey or lost hairs in two of these Ms. "Lacks effort." "Could do better." "Seems to be far away half the time." Which half, I wondered, and how had it been calculated? Their perseverance, however, and that of Mrs Fortune, who gave me extra maths tuition on a window-sill, helped me through. Aided, perhaps, by learning the theory of the shortest distance between two points in dashes down the rainswept farmyard to the lavatory.

My approach to the woodwork teacher's ancient art was, to say the least, wooden. His name deserts me and he wouldn't have wished to remember mine. In future years friends would identify my tools by their rust. For me, a vice was something boys shouldn't talk about, mortise and tenon more a music hall act and dovetail the back end of a pigeon. The master would be entitled to a little mockery. "Right, boy, you may take it home. If you take care it might just hold together till you get there." At least I reckoned that if the legs fell off the buffet on the way home I could pass it off as a teapot stand and two place mats. The buffet did survive longer than predicted but I would only remember *my* bottom risking a sit on it.

Naturally we took kindly to those teachers whose subjects we could manage, which for me were English, French, Latin and History. In English we took turns to give William Shakespeare a Lancashire hearing in class, and that precious stone from John of Gaunt's speech set itself firmly in my mind to surface from its silver sea at unexpected moments of recall. Though I was not taught by Mr Byrom I would long remember his Gallic droning from class to corridor, the nasal voice of France. Did French teachers haunt Montmartre to practise their French? Did Spanish teachers take up flamenco dancing? Would German masters risk a few paces of the goosestep in school halls? In my second year in school the mayor, Alderman Bland, spoke a language which was not on our timetable. It was Esperanto.

Miss Cliff, senior mistress, could freeze with a glare on corridors. It was said that when girls saw her approaching in town they would wipe their shoe toes on the backs of their stockings as a reflex precaution. Yet under her stern exterior pumped a warm heart. It would emerge later that she walked two miles to a farm with chocolates for a girl pupil who had been injured. Though fixed at times by the gaze I was never taught by Miss Cliff, but many valued her English lessons. As a farmer's son the history lesson with animal connections in the Indian Mutiny caught the imagination, the greased paper on cartridges bitten before use. Hindus thought it was grease from the sacred cow and Muslims from the unclean pig, and almost came to riot. Some of the staff seemed to be fixtures in the setting. Herbert Hatch, who wrote geography textbooks, had been on the staff since the Great War. When we were not conjugating or calculating we passed our time in congregating, alliterating, ruminating, perambulating, impersonating, exaggerating, translating, with a little tête-a-têteing, a lot of schoolmating and some unopposed vociferating.

In school assemblies our singing of "Onward Christian Soldiers" carried a calculated risk. Between each verse and chorus the pianist had to rattle out three rising notes and we fell, with little incentive, into the habit of bellowing out One Two Three, giving Gould and Sullivan a simple mathematical dimension we could understand. If the school hadn't been newish it could have had the only academic roof in history to be blown off by three soaring numbers. I would quickly forget most of the words of the school hymn, which lacked a calculating bonus.

Of all the papers our fingers dirtied there were three I dreaded most — examination questions, school reports described with some irony as "terminal" and, worst, summonses to the dentist. The latter were on green paper to match the colour of our cheeks when these missives came through the letter-box. Was it imagination or terror that led us to believe that all dentists had trained with Tommy Farr, studied diplomacy under Genghis Khan and had to top 6 feet to qualify? The medical officer of the time sounded like a teacher. He was a Doctor Markham.

Three bullies overshadowed our peace of mind, two bulky types and a small aggressor who was shorter than some of his prey, though happily nothing physical with me. As general secretary of the society of cowards and crawlers (unpaid) I cultivated an alliance with taller boys and a slick tongue for talking myself out of "Tom Brown corners". My only close encounter, more shadow-boxing than contact, was in a dispute over lockers with another churchgoer and, as his entry into my autograph album would later suggest, a non-aggression pact was drawn up.

Then there were the girls, mentioned only obliquely up to now but without whom the term "mixed school" would have been absurd. We sat in desks next to theirs, borrowed their rulers, competed in examinations, showed off a bit, discussed some film or teacher or outing, opened the odd door for them, picked up a fallen book or two. One day we *noticed* them. More precisely we saw, some of us sooner than others, that they began to fill the school uniforms better than us. They looked neater and cleaner and smelled sweeter for which, being allocated a large nose, I was obliged. In short, they were different. Hey ho, summer had come. X=Y on a desk lid meant something cosier than algebra. There would be whispers and blushes and notes scribbled and passed. There would be giggles and go-betweens, banter, backchat and assignations on the way home. Books would be dropped for a purpose and received with meaningful glances.

It would appear from these notes that my schooldays passed without what was loosely called sport but as with me at team selection time it comes last.

CHAPTER
FIFTEEN

A Team Selector's Nightmare

And greatest dread of all, the dread of games.
John Betjeman

Howzat?
OUT
Dewhurst, stumped 0.

If teachers had asked for an essay on my sporting life I would have been stumped again. A blank page would best reflect my school swimming and cricket achievements. Take water first which, as you now know, was my bête noire (at least the French lessons paid off, Miss Dixon). Water for washing was depressing enough but Bradley Road Baths, pungent, cavernous and tiley, echoed with a carillon of chatter and a trillion mouthfuls of the stuff. To say nothing of earfuls and eyefuls.

Our weekly summons to the baths seemed like some piscatorial revenge for eating fish. As if the swimming bath was not water enough we had pre-immersion rituals, a sort of paddling process followed by a shower. With cold feet in two senses we lined up on the bank like milk jellies, white and shivery. The initiation rite involved leaping out to grab the end of a long pole offered by the inquisitor, sorry, instructor. I doubt whether that pole and me ever made contact and to make things wetter an apprentice sadist shoved me into the deep end and my life flashed before me. Happily, by then it was only a short life and under a sign which clearly shouted Deep End I was hauled to safety. It is unlikely I would have made a better stab at the thing under a Professor of Swimming who had presided over the old public baths in which town water was supplemented by rain water, though I might have grown a bit taller.

I did get some kicks out of football but would have preferred to face next door's bull than a cricket ball. Rain-dancing on cricket afternoons, though tempting, would have taken some nerve in a school where the great Learic Constantine taught the game and caught six out off the bowling of a physics master. For me, the bat was too narrow and the ball like something designed for trench warfare. Though weak in maths I could see no logic in a wide goalmouth for football and three sticks for that other game. All this was a euphemism for cowardice. "Oh sir, we had him last week" was an appeal never more plaintive than when him was me. I had all the white gear, sweater, flannels, boots, but there was no cricketer underneath.

To any who might have asked why all that milk and scrambled egg had produced such an indifferent sportsman I offered one activity in which I was more at home, physical training. One of the PTIs was a strutting figure with a somewhat disciplined régime, and archaeologists may some day unearth a baseball bat which found its way underneath the floorboards of the gymnasium. Whether the bat concentrated mind or behind was for the scientist, but some of us managed ability on ropes and boxes and wall bars. Two of us earned sixpence each for walking across the gym, breadth not length, on our hands, the sort of tanner we preferred. Of course, walking on your hands was not commercially viable unless you were destined for Blackpool Tower Circus. If you showed the gift off to a girl your ice lolly money fell out of your pocket and the hole in your shoe winked at her. As for shoes, there was one extra-mural game that attracted those of us with reasonable eyesight. It was school yard football, played frenetically with a tennis ball through blazer goalposts. The goalkeeper never had a chance and the sport was so damaging to shoe leather that, collectively across the nation, it may have created hundreds of jobs in tanneries.

Some boys excelled in every game and sports day happening and, who knows, in marbles too. Peter Kippax, much senior to me, would go on to play football for Burnley as an amateur and was in a postwar Cup Final with the Clarets. He would also turn out for Burnley at Cricket and at school threw the cricket ball so far that they may still be looking for it. His school yard football must have been dazzling to watch. Though I was never one of those sporting giants to be called out to shake the hand of the VIP on speech day I managed to put enormous energy into applauding the announcement of a day's holiday.

Nothing boosted the morale of a boy more than the sequel to a sports injury, especially if lavishly plastered up, preferably with crutch and seen from a mile away. As a badge of bravery my sports injury was barely noticed on return to school, a slight limp out of all proportion to the pain undergone. "You'll have to go to Shotton," Dad had said — which seemed to promise an outing. But Mr Shotton was a masseur, and was a genius on sprains, strains and other damage. Shotton and another wonder worker in the area, a herbalist with a "well" of coloured cure-all, seemed to pick up all the troubles that the local medical profession hadn't mastered.

I was vanned, limping, to Shotton. His stature for me was enhanced because he was out of town and more so when he linked the damage to football and to a fancy classical name. I'd strained my Achilles tendon connecting heel to calf and stated by a wise book to be often strained by athletes. Athlete. I liked that thought and would bask in its warmth for some time with the added bonus of being absent from several algebra lessons. In years to come I would read the legend. A woman called Thetis plunged her son Achilles into the River Styx to make him safe from wounding. Sadly, the misguided woman held him by the heel which stayed dry and was the weak spot where he was killed by an arrow.

Sport, for Matey, would continue to be a weak spot. Apart from a knockabout at the seaside with a child's bat and a soft ball against primary school opposition I'd never allow cricket to threaten life and limb again. Even football would only be risked when a team was desperate to fill its A.N. Other gap. No idolising would be available from girls for games I would play against a deaf and dumb team in Yorkshire, Indians in their bare feet in Bombay or a team in a Sunday School League game that humbled us with a 22–0 defeat. However, as mother used to say, we must all be good at something and I contrived a reasonable backhand at tennis and could notch eight out of ten for walking, though that was neither gifted nor heroic to most girls — and a waste of time and shoe leather to some.

CHAPTER
SIXTEEN

Hay & Hop Bitters

'Tis haytime and the red-complexioned sun
Was scarcely up 'ere blackbirds had begun
Along the meadow hedges here and there
To sing loud songs to the sweet-smelling air.
John Clare

Our neighbour's farm bracketed the lane from the top
of town to our Little Gib Hill and there was a public
right of way through its yard. With time the yard and its
doorstep dogs became as comforting to me as a favoured
jersey, a hello passing place. Then one afternoon in an
early summer, with the grass lush and tall and the
mowers being oiled for its cutting, I'd heard voices new
to me on the way home from school. Whistling. Low
laughter. Singsong accents I couldn't place drifted from
outbuildings. Our neighbour's farm had been occupied
by Martians. I hurried past hawthorns and wild roses in
the lane and reported to Mother. She wiped floured
hands on her pinafore and smiled at my unknowing.
"They're nothing to worry about. They'll be the
Irishmen, come over to help with the hay."

Dad could tell a Blackburn man from the way he
pronounced certain vowels but we were as unused to

more distant dialects as to wine glasses. So these men from across the Irish Sea were strange to me, though not to the bigger farmers who traditionally hired them. I watched them at work, all back, belt and black trousers as they bent over their scythes, legs apart for balance, to cut the corners of the meadow which mowing machines could not reach. We called it piking.

All across the sweet green meadows of the north the mowing Irishmen would be swaying forward with a semi-circular rhythm as if cutting to music, though strong muscled men would scarcely like the vision of a rural ballet against the green grass and blueish cotton-wool skies, a painter's scene which no box camera black and white could verify. Many boys envied their pace, pausing only to whetstone a scythe, whet a dry whistle, light up, chew baccy or, who knows, share tales or poems of banshees from mother's knee over a peat fire in the auld country.

Only rain stopped hay and when it did some farmers found the men other jobs around the place. Drains. Fences or walls for repair. Drains. Shippons for whitewashing. Drains. Hen-cotes for creosoting. Drains. There was always something sobbing for attention on a farm. Muck spreading was the sire to the hay harvest and like many routines was solitary and monotonous. Apprentices in factories were fair game for leg-pulls, being sent off for a long stand, glass hammer, elbow grease or bucket of steam. Small-scale farming had no such communal mockery but if a farmer attracted an audience of one the quips could fly. A short boy prepared to chance his nose around a muck midden could be advised "Get some of this i' thi clogs. Tha'll shoot up." Muck spreading came in three stages — loading, depositing in heaps, and spreading. Shippon to midden, midden to grass, grass to shippon, a recycling as old as time.

That done, we watched the grass grow and learned to keep off it. We were a family team with no republican support and when Dad anticipated a dry spell and gave the thumbs-up for our making hay the four of us were on standby. Some farmers kept older sons off school for haytime, a mixed blessing for the boys as even algebra produced less sweat. Tractors, new-fangled contraptions, were for the big men. Our grassland cycle was ably supported on the withers of Jinny or Billy, which never declined to start on damp mornings or run out of fuel on the last quarter of an acre. Our neighbours used traditional two-wheeled carts with extra shelving back and front. Our hay came in on Billy's flat cart or by Jinny, prayer and sledge, primitive but useful in hilly places. The sledge-runners were smoother than the glass of the hop bitters and sarsaparilla cooling under haycocks. The Irishmen were perhaps primed by ale. We, a family of abstainers, refreshed ourselves with soft drinks, including dandelion and burdock. Hop bitters suggested that our hay might be cut in wavy lines but the drink was strictly TT. Haymaking was labour intensive and thirsty work but more critically in a damp climate it was prey to the weather. Judgement, graft, luck and prayer were all required to prevent the hay from being ruined and for Dad that list would begin with prayer. We worked against frowning skies to make sure our stock had winter dinners and sometimes ate an al fresco picnic from haybox cooker in the meadow.

I was too young to mow with horse but was allowed to risk removal of a toe with scythe. Dad had sole control of the mowing machine but one day, ironically on the flat meadow, horse and driver overturned, happily without injury to either. The same topsy-turvy accident on another neighbour's round hill would have been more serious. He seemed to slant at 45 degrees on his machine without toppling over. The green swathes were turned by hand rakes to dry underneath and by then aunts and uncles would be in the process and I thought competent enough to lead one of the lines of rakers. Next, the grass was shaken out by two-prong forks for more drying, then raked into a hamlet of haycocks, like igloos. Heaps were joined together for loading, known as "leading". I would be propped on the sledge to accept forkfuls, one each side and one in the middle for wedging like keystones in a wall. Riding high had one setback — a redheaded boy could be punished by a midday sun, and one year I'd blisters like halves of soft eggs on the shoulders, for once unprotected.

Hay, gathered in when too damp, could risk combustion and possible barn fire and I used to lie awake overhearing my parents discuss the chance even though Dad had done his test of plunging his fist into a haycock to check dampness. When all was gathered in I used to pray for rain, convinced that if the barn caught fire a downpour would put it out. Thankfully, we never had a fire though some farmers were less fortunate. Any snaps of Jinny hauling hay by sledge did not survive but one of Billy in his flat cart showed him besieged by mother, dad, an uncle, two aunts and whoever took the snap. The load, barely big enough to feed two cows, had me perched on top like a paperweight. The seven, plus me, amounted to a great blessing of labour that day. After the last load of summer the meadows shone light green against the olive of hedges. Some farmers left a dark green oasis where, with a countryman's compassion, they'd mown around a nest with sitting tenants. Haymaking in some Lancashire summers could be heartbreaking. In dry weather it was congenial and rewarding but always *work*. Dad could have been forgiven in the mid-thirties keep-fit craze for muttering: "Let 'em come and make hay. We'll keep 'em fit and they'll be doing summat useful at same time." Certainly, an hour with fork or rake in warm sunshine could knock off a few ounces and neither Mother nor Dad had any surplus weight.

CHAPTER
SEVENTEEN

A Windfall of
Uncles & Aunties

But pleasures are like poppies spread
You seize the flow'r, its bloom is shed
or like the snow falls in the river
a moment white, then melts for ever.
Robert Burns

Dunnow Hall played hide and seek in a wood above the River Hodder in Yorkshire. We were privy to its genteel charm because an uncle and aunt lived in a house in its courtyard. Uncle Harold, motor cyclist and a horsepower buff for whom the combustion engine was invented, was working as an electrician on a new reservoir in the district and to cushion the men's isolation would show them early films on a cinematograph. The reservoir swallowed up a hamlet, twenty cottages, a shop and post office.

The Victorian turreted hall itself was on the outskirts of Slaidburn village, and in my early childhood we'd chug from Lancashire on a motor cycle and sidecar or milk van with less angst than travellers from the past. The machine coughed around Pendle Hill through

102

communities where women were accused of witchcraft in the early seventeenth century. Snug on mother's knee I was too young to know of the grisly cartings through the forests of Pendle and Bowland of wretched women being driven to trial at Lancaster where seven at least were hanged. Only later did the tales of Demdikes and Chattoxes turning ale sour and bewitching superstitious villagers cast shadows on life, and how much of it was down to fear, distrust or revenge left decades of doubt behind. Although we passed a witch's grave, the "eye of God" in a church wall and a gibbet site near Pendle Hill where a highwayman was said to have been hanged, our cross-boundary jaunts were threatened only by weather, a stray sheep or two, a minor overturning on a hairpin bend overlooking Slaidburn, one of those stiff climbs for the old cars that Dad and Uncle would boil over about.

We saw no witches, though an occasional drenched hiker could have passed for one. From the hairpin we crossed the Hodder into stone-grey Slaidburn with its thirteenth-century Hark to Bounty Inn, renamed from a parson who used to leave his dog Bounty outside and when it barked say "Hark to Bounty". It was a charming explanation and we hoped it was not just a shaggy dog story. We found the hall down a twisted wooded track. A line, pegged with magpies, crows, stoats and other predators, showed up, the first I'd seen, the game-keeper's inventory of his cull to show he was earning his keep.

The hall, as remembered, was furnished but unoccupied. Uncle Harold and Auntie Gladys's house was linked by door to its spacious billiard hall where my cousin Marian and a neighbour's son were allowed to motor around a full-sized table in pedal cars and there may, for my parents at least, have been a feeling of eaves-dropping on the gentry. Children remember the least predicted, and an image of coloured glass lit by sunshine and rainbowing the hallway stayed with me. In late winter a large tree near a tennis court was underswept with snowdrops. My cousin used to go off to the village school with her egg sandwiches for a year or two before they moved from the village. Our direction changed and we began to visit the Carmans closer to Preston. Uncle worked as electrician to the Whittingham Hospital for mentally troubled patients, and on summer saunters with him in its spacious grounds he would nod amiably and speak on first-name terms to residents who were allowed freedom of the grounds and, for some, of the village, Goosnargh. "Good morning, Doctor," one might say to him, recognising Uncle but not his role in the place. Slight disarrangements of dress or some telltale odd question would give the game away.

One afternoon we'd motored for the first time to blustery moors above Cragg Vale, Mytholmroyd, in another corner of Yorkshire, to meet two round relations, an aunt and uncle with the prefix great. Mytholmroyd, I would learn in years to come, was the birthplace of Ted Hughes, whose poems on stone walls would key in with my impression of Keilham, great-uncle Fred's holding in the clouds. His farm never saw our van. We had to leave it where a lane ran out and trudge on tracks in an area in which the Cragg Vale coiners, eighteenth-century forgers of the moors, clipped golden guineas to re-strike as Portuguese pieces, a counterfeiting that cost their leader, "King David", his head in execution at York.

As we approached Keilham Uncle's black and tan dog publicised us from a distance. Callers were rare and its bark of caution brought Fred and Esther, two ample bodies, one waistcoated, one pinafored, to their gate to welcome us. Uncle Fred, like many of his generation, wore trousers that almost hugged his chest and the mandatory wide peaked cap over his rose-red face. Theirs was the only cat's whisker set I ever saw. Two pot dogs sat on their dresser and both of them and their live cousin outside stayed mute while I, a mischievous four or five, filled the great-uncle's water trough with stones. They had, after all, called it a stone trough.

One of the more regular closer-to-home outings was to another farm where another well in the yard supplied water for house and animals. Auntie Annie, at Sabden Fold, spread home-made teas for visitors with such warmth and quality that some became close friends. The canine receptionist there was Uncle Albert's dog Jock, and I would specially remember cousin Doris for pram-pushing me to see a monkey in Nelson market. In school holidays I'd stay with Uncle Wilson and Auntie Elsie at their newsagents', sweets and various items store in Barwick-in-Elmet, near Leeds, with a maypole dancing tradition. Uncle delivered newspapers by sturdy bicycle on calendar picture lanes and used to allow me to cycle with him to explore Yorkshire drives and letter boxes. In winter he parcelled inside his trouser legs with brown paper against Yorkshire rain. An early bus would deposit *Yorkshire Posts* and other daily newspapers to permeate the shop with printers' ink. More memorably, on Sunday mornings my cousins Kenneth and Cyril and I could choose sweets from stoppered bottles on the counter on our way to the Methodist chapel, a sweeter lure to worship than sermon or hymns, the latter accompanied ultimately by Kenneth, with Cyril blowing the organ. Some of these uncles were the last generation of the cut-throat-razor-strop men, skilled in the hazardous rite though, as wisps of newsprint on facial errors would show, not entirely infallible.

Farming is an all-seasons halter for the farmer and holidays were not often possible. Mother and I stayed once in a village near Blackpool for B and B at the home of the local blacksmith, but the generous helpings of holiday were when dad took us off for a choppy voyage on boats like *Snaefell, King Orry* and *Lady of Man* for a week among his relatives on the Manx isle. Uncle Arnold was Dad's cousin. He was a gem. With a leg handicap from childhood he'd gone with his parents and sisters from Nelson to Laxey. It was said that at first Manx children used to knock on their door to hear his mother's Lancashire accent. At one time they lived in the cosily named Social Cottage but moved to a detached house overlooking the Irish Sea with an ankle-testing path to the beach, where in summers to come we'd spend holidays with Arnold's sister Celia and family.

Arnold married a local girl, Renee, and turned his hand to baking and butchering. He had a wry sense of humour and I long saw him with cigarette on lip and, again, the obligatory wide peaked cap, cutting peat on a moor for his open fires. Local people had a named plot of peat and a gentleman's agreement to keep to their own. Arnold had various gifts. He played violin in a small orchestra in one of the glens, painted landscapes and navigated small, unpredictable boats out of Laxey Harbour with a dog passenger. Was it only apocryphal that one of the dogs on his *King Orry* or *Ariel* had a brief encounter with the engine and joined the official Manx cat in having no tail? Arnold's credentials with me were enhanced when he stopped his bakery van on a fuchsia lane where we were walking and handed me a fresh cream bun out of the back. Boys remembered fat cream cakes.

Auntie Martha had dark hair parted down the centre and tight to her head. She was friend and adviser to me in her time at the farm and sometimes accomplice in minor mischiefs, and I would share some close secrets, nothing too important, until I was ready to give them to Mother and Dad. She would share some of hers with me, though only small ones. She used to search out the unusual or the very ordinary for presents. Indoor fireworks gave her a special fizz but the others had some reservations about the smells and residue from them which could pass for the deposits of domestic animals. With her, the old chestnut about a bag of nuts

107

and a balloon for Christmas once achieved reality. She would come up with such clichés for jokey gifts.

Auntie was a member of a gospel mission where young ladies wore uniform berets and smocks. Her Bible was well-thumbed, with, as remembered, coloured edges for easy reference. It was common to see her reading by lamplight, and tracts and bookmarks on scriptural themes would spill from her handbag and pockets. It was a time when itinerant evangelists like Gypsy Smith or Pastor Jeffreys would set up their causes in the district and count on followers glowing up with friends, Testaments in hand, for the testimonies, choruses, messages and saving of souls. Auntie would take holidays in Christian guesthouses for gospel meetings and on one postcard, from Southport, would write of hearing a Mr Sutcliffe preach. He spoke until 9.25 and she missed her supper, but wasn't hungry. Ultimately a family album would have in its closing pages at least a dozen pastors and missionaries, almost like an epilogue.

Uncle Harold and Auntie Jessie in Barrowford had embarked on what would become a family of seven children and would bless their home with laughter and tears and a carillon of voices. We were always warmly welcomed into the family atmosphere, a cup of sweet tea arriving from somewhere. In the coming war uncle would leave for the army and be at Arnhem from where a letter home would enquire about the family's Brussels sprouts. There were none and the little ruse would cast some doubt on Army censors. Uncle would become a preacher in Independent Methodism and oblige with a tenor solo at times from the pulpit.

On our days out Mother would spy out some farm or cottage on a skyline and link it to her family, cousin so-and-so and great-uncle whatsisname. It seemed as if our family were inheriting the earth and we were not alone among families on the Lancashire-Yorkshire boundary who claimed to have been related to, befriended by or simply "played out" with Philip Snowden, future Labour Chancellor of the Exchequer, from the Cowling area just inside Yorkshire. One relative owned a small cinema in Burnley, another was headmistress of a small school in the Yorkshire Dales and Great-uncle Jack farmed beneath the scramble track up Pendle Hill.

There were two Great-uncle Wilfreds. One, a greengrocer and member of the Poultry Club, would become something impressive in the ARP, and his wife, Auntie Clara, in the St John Ambulance Brigade. The other, an amiable tenor singer distinguished in wing collar or bow tie (uncharacteristic of Nelson), was more impressive in oratorio and on concert platforms. Wilfred Hindle was a company secretary but I used to think that he sang for his living because that was what we saw him doing. At future Christmases we would be entertained around well-stocked table and fires at the home he shared with Auntie Edith Alice, known as Deedie, and son Tom. Uncle would play gramophone records to us and share an eternal problem of "raining in" through a rear window but rarely sang to us there. To hear his rich round rising notes you had to sit near him in our family pew, listen to his recitatives from the choir stalls or share his lyrical thoughts in concerts on the precise identity of Sylvia ("Who is she?"), the perfection of the English rose or his generous offer of the keys of heaven. He seemed modest about his success. Only in years to come, from others, would I learn that he sang across the north-west, broadcast several times dating back to the old BBC and 2LO and was accompanied in an early concert by Mr Gerald Bright, who became Geraldo. He won many trophies for singing, taught it, and, someone said, always carried a couple of songs in his attaché case to oblige and "bring cheer". He made personal records of ballads with Columbia Records and one with His Master's Voice with Nipper the dog on the label.

As a boy I was perhaps more focused on Great-uncle Jack who sold tripe and pies from a little shop in Burnley and created spiralling smoke signals with his pipe and matchbox. Boys would be inclined to remember smoke signals longer than the tallest notes of the Hallelujah Chorus.

CHAPTER
EIGHTEEN

Grandmas Mainly

For a boy with a galloping dislike of water it was of passing interest that both of my grandmas lived in streets with a wettish label. My Dad's mother had a terraced house in Fountain Street in Nelson and my maternal grandmother occupied the middle of three in Ford Street, Barrowford. The first probably got its name from the town's Kew Gardens, where years before local people used to throw twopence each into a wheelbarrow for the privilege of seeing balloon ascents, racing and jumping. Ford Street, like the village name, took its title from old fords across the river there.

Watery connections aside, there were other similarities between the two women. Both had two first names, one each from the Scriptures to which they were devoted, both had blessed me with a generous helping of baking aunts and each of their homes concealed a well of spice (toffees) which never seemed to dry up, and the prospect of sardines on toast, a Matey favourite. Sarah Ellen Dewhurst, my Nelson grandma, was a plump, huggable soul with a round-as-moon face. She had been Sunday School teacher and member of the choir and women's class at Salem Chapel which was up the main street from her last home. I liked to visit her but whether that was entirely mutual was uncertain. "I could do with Ernest but he ronces on t'settee," she complained to an aunt. I never found the meaning of the verb "to ronce" though it would have something to do with fidgeting and the crumpling of newly ironed covers. (The trespass of roncing would be recycled in family gossip down the years along with the legends of the boil-on-the-slide lancing, cowpat hurling and of Matey, at six months, being privileged to hold the keys of York Minster in his podgy hands, briefly and memorably, on a family visit to the cathedral.) My grandma would refer to the RC faithful rather tartly as "Carthlics" and perhaps this tainted me. I would walk past the "Carthlic" churches in town with some wariness as if I could be drawn into mysterious and ornamental rites. How naive we were!

Anglican churches were only slightly more apparent than RC ones, but chapels and missions seemed to have seeded everywhere, big, medium, small, on street corners or in the centre of town, and catering for a spectrum of free church faith and practice. Chapels where the great John Wesley preached were within walking distance for the old preachers who would trudge miles to pulpit appointments.

My maternal grandma, Esther Jane Hargreaves, a farmer's daughter, leaned more towards gospel services, member of a local mission but prepared to drop in, sometimes late, on other fellowships. She was a hardworking Christian woman who reared six children after her husband's early death and saw most of them anchored in the faith. An early snapshot showed her with her then unmarried five daughters, three brunettes and two redheads with a bias to Mary Pickford hairstyles. Any photographer peering through his lens at Grandma was likely to find flowers clutched in her hand, in a buttonhole or trimming a hat. Her secondary belief was in the fundamental powers of various alleged remedies with somewhat unsociable tastes and, for me, doubtful benefits. Was it then, or later, that we were initiated into the fellowship of Dutch drops, taken on a sugar lump incentive, and Liquefruta, taken without bribe, and various others whose names and foulness are thankfully forgotten?

Grandma Hargreaves kept fishing nets for my cousins and me to trawl the park lake or the water's edge across the road, not far from where a character named Billy Blacksmith blew his worthy bellows. On her parlour window-sill outside the front of the house she kept two large seaside shells in which we were invited to listen to the sea — all of which added up to a substantial amount of water for someone allergic to it.

I only knew one of my grandfathers and then only for a short time. Ernest, the butcher turned farm auctioneer, whose name I inherited, had died long before I was born. My paternal grandfather, John Henry, was a tall gangling man with a fulsome moustache, a choir member who sadly struggled with acute deafness that called for loud bellowing into his ear. My lasting memory of him was the tower of toast he used to erect on the hearth. Boys remembered buttered toast.

CHAPTER
NINETEEN

Grandma's 'Do'
& the Winter Scene

Treasure your families — the future of humanity passes by way of the family.

John Paul II

The evening of Christmas Day. Fountain Street as empty as Santa's sack between grey terraced rows. A hint of frost. Christmas had crept indoors, and behind the closed curtains of number 19 Grandma's family squeezed around a parlour blaze as snug and cheerful as crackers in a box and with as many stock jokes. We were at Grandma Dewhurst's annual "do" with herself at the hub twiddling her thumbs on her lap and trying to keep tuned to the network of gossip. "Who's Armstrong, did she say?" Another round of nuts or dates, another shovelful on the fire and the turns and games began.

"What is it this year? Walter de la Mare again?" There was nowhere to hide from Auntie Florrie's organising gaze. "It'll be 'Sea Fever', Auntie." Walter had seemed to haunt my life and this time I would give him a sabbatical. You could almost hear the uncles groaning like schooners as I offered up some of the salty Masefield. Nut-cracking paused and they managed a corked hearing of the poem. Such undemanding moments were a breather for them from Auntie's list of party games to which they would adhere somewhat loosely — stations, pencil and paper games and a regular called apple apple apple in which a fruit was repeated three times before someone could shout it out once. Some bright spark would choose loganberry to outdo opponents and after turkey and hearth-warmed mince pies loganberry *once* was a mouthful. If family events had not been alcohol-free even cherry cherry cherry would have strangled language. One forfeit was to bite an inch off a poker which lost its novelty for all except newcomers when the secret was known. The poker had to be held an inch away from the mouth as the teeth bit into fresh air. Adults were not usually asked to perform though Dad could impress by mouthing the name of a Welsh railway station with 58 letters in it. What's more, he'd been there.

Grandma's annual shindig was like a breakfast gong calling all the family to dine. Auntie Florrie, schoolteacher, cyclist and walker, in hand-knitted slippers and cardigan, was an enthusiast who prepared our games studiously and was obvious choice for organiser. Her games eased boredom for the nephews who could be asked by uncles to "go to t' top of Colne for an icecream". Colne was two miles away on a rising slope and on Christmas Day was as closed up as a boxer's eye. They knew *their* money was safe and we knew their game.

115

Auntie Florrie was a slim directory of flora and place names from cycle jaunts and walking tours with husband Edgar and was well researched when she shepherded her infant children on rural walks. "A guelder rose? Yes, there's one down a lane near Gisburn." Gentle enough but we heard she could silence a boy with one hand while vamping out the morning march into the school hall with the other. "Spring forward, fall back" was her Americanised rule for remembering the seasonal adjustment of clocks. In visits to her home I looked for the big encyclopaedia and the washing-of-hands rite before absorbing its knowledge. Chocolates were distributed sparingly and the mothball enhancement of her stored boxes made her somehow more endearing.

While one of my aunts read detective thrillers and some others only religious books Auntie Florrie nourished herself on northern regional novels which revisited her haunts — the Brontës, Harrison Ainsworth's *Lancashire Witches*, Phyllis Bentley, Halliwell Sutcliffe and the "Windyridge" novels of W. Riley. I was blessed with an abundance of "real" aunts and others who came by adoption, and became a competent judge of their chocolate cakes and biscuits. One of my indirect aunts used to perform with actions a rhyme which went

> I am a teapot
> Here's my spout
> Here's my handle
> Pour me out.

It was a fleeting amusement for a sit-still boy on a wet afternoon though the actress, being tall rather than teapot-shaped, would have been better cast for a coffee pot rhyme. Her husband was special in my affections. He carried a Fry's chocolate bar or mints in his pocket.

While the term auntie suggested close relationship the aunts minus the ie were usually older, perhaps more austere and remote. It was said that I used to groan when it was announced that we were to visit *the aunts*, two rather stately ladies who lived together, though I never felt ill at ease in their presence. Aunt Margaret (known as Margit) and Alice Ann seemed fond of black and were upright in both senses as if disciplined by corsetry, and suitably braided, buttoned and beaded with nothing out of place or character. I would not have dared to utter the word corsetry in their hearing.

Grandma's party was one of winter's perks and even Dad was lured away from the farm for half a day. Another boy-treat was bonfire night, more specially the week before it, when Dad would jolly home with a box of fireworks. The shapes and colours and promised performance were like a sneaked peep at the fairyland to come, and I had more fun looking at the snowstorms, rockets, catherine wheels and little demons in red jackets than the flash of ignition. Penny-for-the-Guy was for town but Mother made plot toffee and Dad sacrificed some of their heirloom wood he'd been saving for a rainy day. Sometimes it *was* a rainy day. We shook sparklers, and roasted potatoes in the dying fire, and next day canvassed the ashes for skeletal metal and sniffed burnt-out firework cases.

Town children would be hunting for black coins from the innards of burnt suites. We got continuity of joy out of Guy Fawkes.

We gave much time to cigarette cards, cartoon characters and comics like *Film Fun, Comic Cuts* and later the *Hotspur, Beano* and *Dandy*, absorbing the doings of Korky the Cat, Pip, Squeak and Wilfred, Frosty McNab, the Freezy Wheeze Man, Desperate Dan, and Japhet and Happy of the *News Chronicle* whose 1935 annual with an ostrich with a sore throat on the cover was on the bookshelf. Such names lingered, only partly overtaken in years to come by the inventions of Dickens — Pumblechook, Turveydrop, Pecksniff, Nubbles and Grip, Barnaby's raven. Churchmans offered cigarette cards on boxers, Players on aircraft and garden flowers but there was no call for them in the boys' yards. In 1935 stars like Tom Walls and Joan Bennett beamed from Gallaghers' packets and perhaps Dad's hen-keeping was fired in part by Ogdens' poultry-rearing series in the twenties. The card craze may have kept half the town's dads puffing away like Puffing Billy, a motor train which paused at a halt somewhere below the farm. After twenty years of puffing, Billy got wheezier and gave way to a push-and-pull train and went off to Wakefield to do more puffing like some dads, whose habit would extend the groaning season for a tame joke:

Boy in shop: Have you any Wild Woodbines?
Shopkeeper: Yes, sonny, we have.
Boy: Why don't you try taming 'em then?

Our chapel, some thought, had been used to show some of the early films which flickered away in our town. We were not regular patrons of picture houses with their flashlight guides, timpani of tip-up seats and partial slink to exits during the standstill anthem, but would find time for recommended films. Dad made George Formby's film *No Limit* about the TT races a must but sensed some sort of busman's holiday when the cockerel crowed at him from Pathé Gazette. *Oh Mr Porter!* rib-tickled us all with Will Hay, a station washing-line, hens and Moore Marriott announcing that "Next train's gone".

Cowboys came galloping through childblare cinemas. Boys used to joke that they'd seen Tom Mix in *Cement* and wait for the groan. The old black-and-white westerns used the same props, sets and casts and trees for galloping by. Ex-opera singers crooned from horseback. Lone Rangers were misnamed. They had sidekicks, breeches and neckties. Sheriffs were pushovers and heroines blonde and dumb in sweaters. Dialogue could be forecast. "No, Martha, we're in the right." "There's some things a man can't take." "Fella must have left in a hurry. He's run out of his pants." Mexicans were losers who might have had more luck if they'd avoided inverted sentences. "They would hang me by the neck and that I would not like." Frail old men were prone to eviction and heroes had to be on white horses and in white hats which declined to fall off in fights. If the lead could sing and the blonde applaud and shout "bravo, bravo" so much the cornier.

Orchestras would start up from a vast prairie at the drop of a hat, black or white.

Heroes came to us in comics, through pocket money, through the school yard swap-and-haggle system and also in books which found us in Sherwood Forest, on Treasure Island or with John Ridd on Exmoor. For presents or Sunday School prizes we'd opt for comic annuals or the boys of children's literature, Tom Brown, Jack Hawkins or that other Brown, the liquorice water kid and leader of the intrepid Outlaws, arch-enemy of she of the lithp, Violet Elizabeth Bott, who expected to be firtht because her father was rich. I often shared William Brown's dirty face and dislike of its cure. He had a mongrel dog. We had two. His arithmetic was vile. I was certain he "ronced" on his grandmother's settee and some of his lip was envied. "She's a real Botticelli," the young man said. "Bottled cherry yourself," William said. I had one possession which to my knowledge Richmal Crompton never gave to William — a brown monkey, a woolly glove puppet with which I would offer free entertainment over the back of a chair to anyone who was willing to humour me.

CHAPTER
TWENTY

Bread of Heaven

Christ is the foundation
Of the house we raise.
J.S.B. Monsell

Salem, our family chapel with its tower, galleries and pews for 900, stood in the town centre. It dwarfed the traffic and gave a shoppers' guard of honour to brides who stepped out of its grey portico in the pinkblush of marriage. Somewhere in it were those memorial stones, one laid by my great-grandfather for the chapel's trustees as the nineteenth century was slipping away. He said he was glad the stones were for a chapel and not a brewery, public house, gambling den or workhouse and received a silver trowel to hand down to his descendants.

The chapel was lofty, wide and brown inside, awesome almost to a child who could take the ceiling for heaven and believe it was literally God's house. As trams racketed down Scotland Road I was taken there first for baptism, nursed in pews for special services and as a toddler-on-knee-fidget muffled with caramels or silver mints with a polar bear on the wrappers. From boyhood to youth and beyond I would watch the preaching wing of the Independent Methodist democracy at work from our rented family pew off the left aisle and perhaps envied boys who could lean over the front of the gallery and try to link bald heads and women's hats to their owners.

Our chapel, like others in Independent Methodism, had an unpaid ministry of men and women and other preachers on its Plan who were not ministers. There were no elevating gowns or titles. A different face looked down from the pulpit each Sunday, sometimes two in one day, and preachers ranged on a sermon Beaufort Scale from moderate through variable to Force Nine. They came in all shapes and sizes and tones of voice with a variety of sermons and presentation styles. Some clutched the pulpit for support. Some leaned over it and lowered the voice at times. A fervent evangelical, eyes lit with zeal, would shout Hallelujah without warning and reclaim any dozers. Others would travel the pulpit and supplement the message with arm gestures and the occasional test of its woodwork. Elevation for short preachers was available on a pulpit box. Most preachers, inevitably, were stationary and largely undramatic. Fidgeting was guaranteed when a preacher with seven points to his sermon and sustained by sips of water from the pulpit glass announced his fifth after twenty-five minutes. More cosily, short interludes for children were included, based on a Bible story, anecdote or visual aid. If a child's mind strayed he, or she, could count the choir, the visible pipes on the great organ (twenty-nine) the number of jokes, sips of water or poundings on the pulpit.

There we sat in Sunday best before preachers who were a microcosm of the town — teachers, housewives, clerks, mill workers, trade unionists, shopkeepers, farmers. Public and political life was represented in pulpit and congregation and in years to come we would learn that the town's first mayor had worshipped in our previous building before leaving us for the Wesleyans. We were in a fellowship which gave the town three mayors, an argument of councillors and two Labour MPs, both ministers of the chapel. Historically, its premises had been used to launch local movements and needs in the growing workaday town. Our founders had left Primitive Methodism because of its authoritarian ministry and the cause they founded in old handloom rooms, the Dandy Shop, blossomed into the biggest church building in Independent Methodism. Hymn-singing to clarinet and fiddle gave way to the new pipe organ. Some would tell that the early faithful at one of our neighbouring Colne chapels had been primed for hymns by Mr James Hartley ("Happy") who whistled their tunes for them before the fellowship aspired to a violoncello.

Ours was a traditional hymn sandwich service, with Charles Wesley outdoing all other writers in the hymnbook. We could sing for every need from the return of backsliders to anticipation of heaven.

For backsliders.
Return O wanderer return
And seek an injured Father's face.

For temperance:
Sail on for morning cometh
The port you yet shall win
And all the bells of God shall ring
The ship of temperance in.
(No *double entendre* intended on the word "port")

For anticipations of heaven:
O for the robes of whiteness
O for the tearless eyes
O for the glorious brightness
Of the unclouded skies.

Sunday best, bought for a wedding perhaps, would appear first for a special service, and for men was usually a dark suit. A light jacket would glow in church like a Christmas candle.

Longfellow, Tennyson and Anne Brontë gave literary status to some of our singing. Hymns were gloomy or bright or something in between and some had tiresome words for boys like paraclete, starry host, seraph and whited sepulchres. Harps, gates, crowns and lamps recurred. The faithful could arrive on a wet Sunday morning to "Sweet is the sunshine after rain" and in the evening be "plunged in a gulf of dark despair".

Salem chapel had a substantial choir and congregation at the time. The bread of heaven would rise from Cwm Rhondda with a swell the Welsh might have envied, the men's notes surging like breakers off Anglesey. Feed me now and evermore, and E V E R M O R E. The choir had its own soloists but called on outsiders for oratorios. Special services, attracting more wool on seats and outbreaks of new millinery, covered everything from missionaries to men and women (separately) and flowers. People used to say "It'll be fine on Sunday, it's Salem 'charity'", as if the anniversary had a concession from Above. John Pickup, elocutionist, elegant in grey suit and perhaps matching spats, had recited from *Silas Marner* and from "Enoch Arden", Tennyson's poem of a shipwrecked boatswain and his wife Anne who misinterprets a text for his presence in heaven and marries another. John Duxbury, another elocutionist, travelled from London, possibly in spats, to recite *The Strange Case of Dr Jekyll and Mr Hyde*, though not on the Sabbath of course.

More to our taste as boys were the harvest teas founded on the fruit and vegetable displays in chapel on Harvest Sunday. For a cotton town shuttles and shirts might have blended more than fruit and veg and blooms but Matey had no complaints, cotton being uneatable. Plunging for the umpteenth time into "We plough the fields and scatter" we counted the hours to tea Tuesdays when food surplus to the needs of the sick and elderly was made available for the hale and hearty, just reward for frowning over algebra homework before the boiled veg and stewed apples were dished up by a (s)mothering of pinafored mothers and grans.

Salem was a pioneer in total abstinence and once the borough bellman in his gold-buttoned coat had been sent round to announce temperance meetings, but our invitations came through the church notices and we were urged to sign a pledge to shun the demon drink.

125

Our Band of Hope was the last of its kind in town and the movement, poverty and other restraints would have some impact, for in 1951 Nelson would be the town drinking the least amount of beer per head in the country, an irony for a town named after the Nelson Inn. Certainly, poverty had lurked behind many doors and in the early thirties the chapel was giving out food parcels, toys and money to families in need and coal to the poor and elderly.

The Band of Hope was organised eventually, as remembered, by Arthur Bolton who, in chapel services, shed a glow from his face whoever the preacher or whatever his text. For Arthur, only good could come out of Nazareth. His contemporaries on the church committee included Alderman Joseph Husband, tiny newsagent and minister, and Alderman Joseph Robinson whose mind could be as sharp as the church secretary's minutes pencil in church meetings. "Point of order, brother." Both aldermen served as mayors. Edgar Barrett, church secretary at the time, had fresh, almost boyish looks, a roundness of face and figure that left him no obvious rivals for an annual manifestation as Father Christmas. Dad, who would be recruited to deputise in that benevolence once, presented a smaller, leaner Santa, suggesting a famine in Lapland.

The name Salem, suggested by its first woman preacher, meant peace, and though its members served voluntarily in the Great War, many never to return, others registered as conscientious objectors and some went to prison for their stand, including two of my uncles.

Chapels, especially rambling places like ours, had a hunger for money to meet maintenance and running costs and one source was the chapel jumble sale. If on holiday from school I would help to "clutter up" this rummaging, and stand expectantly by some stall in the hope that a passing aunt would stump up for a model car with one wheel missing or a *Film Fun* comic with a copper off for jam stains on Stan Laurel's face. Everything from clocks and cardies to copies of "The Bluebells of Scotland" passed the price-assessing women before a floodtide of bargain hunters washed away any untethered toddlers. Some assessments were made for the benefit of potential buyers "in-house". "Hey, I know that coat. She's only worn it twice and not to chapel. It's too tight around the hips." Or "a reight good bargain that old clock. It's Jimmy's. Sez it only needs a screw and a bit of fiddling wi' and it'll keep better time than Big Ben." With little to spare in some homes jumble sales were a social service. Leftovers were carted off to the local marine stores, known affectionately as t'rag shop. Whether or not I acquired a tear-stained copy of *Smallwood's Tutor for the Pianoforte* from one of the jumble piles was not recorded.

The church committee employed a scribe, unpaid like all except Mr Kenyon, the caretaker, to immortalise its doings. One report covered a visit from a Mr Verney Phillips with a challenging discourse on "the present tendency to paganism". Deaths were reported under visits from The Reaper, the Angel of Death, or on a passing to the Great Beyond, which must have sounded like a million miles to children who'd never travelled further than Catlow Bottoms for a picnic. As children, we'd much to learn, not least from adult euphemisms aimed at softening the blow but sometimes making things worse. Anyone moved to tears was said to have "filled up" as if a reservoir of tears had overflowed. Passed away. Gone to his reward. Gone to Glory. Gone home. It was not unusual to overhear in a street "I lost mi husband last month" as if the deceased was only temporarily mislaid and for Christians, with eternity in their sights, that was scripturally and surely so.

CHAPTER
TWENTY-ONE

Ghosts on Cardboard

A photograph is a secret about a secret.
The more it tells you the less you know.
Diane Arbus, US photographer

Like Dad, with his stored wood, Mother clung to this
and that, little gems to nudge her memory —
newspaper cuttings, recipes, pressed wild flowers,
quotations, thoughts and homilies that lifted her spirits.
If the barn had caught fire (rural equivalent of the
Clapham omnibus) she'd have hurried from the
farmhouse with not the family silver, since there was
none, but with family snaps. Many of these, especially
from Mother's side, found their way into drawers and
cupboards, an old suitcase under the bed and dusty
albums with slits to hold them in place. They haunted
us, these ghosts from the past, dusted down at times
and puzzled over. Some would remain as vague to us as
figures in a mist.

That seven-piece hirsute orchestra of Victorian
worthies, for instance, tagged only by the scribbled
word on the back: Sam Hargreaves, second from left,
with a violin under his arm, and by that brief note
fixed into Mother's side of the family. Three more

violinists, uniform in waistcoat and watch chains, were there, and two viola players, seniors, and one with beard round as a roly-poly pudding. Centred, a man with pointed beard and a plaque, the leader/conductor perhaps. We longed for them to come off the print and bless the room with Mozart.

A horse was pictured in two poses, prone as if dead, and seated with his trainer using him as a sofa. Another horse in a milk float posed with a handsome milkman, moustached as all, probably Grandad's neighbour in Blacko. A group under a horse-chestnut tree featured Grandma Hargreaves, three children, a watch-chained old man with bird's nest beard and a short man, perhaps a farm hand, and all seven in clogs.

Two images of maternal Grandad were inherited, one with Grandma and their first four children in a doorway. More poignantly, a portrait of him on which was crayoned "Annie's daddy, poor daddy", sad reference to a man who died too young. Later Annie herself was photographed as May Queen of Barrowford village, in bullnosed car with mock courtiers.

So they came down to us, young bloods with watch chains, white collars and ties and peeping pocket handkerchiefs, girls in buttoned-up boots, a woman in a long tight-waisted dress and not a hand-down name among them. Who was missing, camera in hand, from that family picnic with hamper and singing kettle on primus, teapots and tablecloth spread on grass? What was in the Gladstone bag? Again, men in boaters and boys in caps like space-ships pictured on a canal boat trip and, much later, a gospel mission outing of thirty-six women and one pastor in front of their motor coach. The pastor was the only one without a hat.

CHAPTER
TWENTY-TWO

Countdown

This war, like the next one, is the war to end war.
David Lloyd George

Tum Hill was as unsuited to cricket as Holland to mountaineering so it was fitting that there was no cricketer inside me knocking to come out. Haytime arrived with the cricket season, and topography and timing together made a nobler excuse than cowardice for opting out of our national game. I was neither player nor spectator of the sport and though Dad had more interest than me we were not seen much on Nelson cricket ground in the thirties, though it would be wrong to suggest that the club did not have great incentives for its faithful.

Apart from the lures of the great Learie Constantine, cricketing legend, and the town's championship team, the gravitational pull at home matches was towards one Nighty, Sunday name Mr Alwyn Nightingale, whose humorous heckling and barbed critiques of play drew his own fan club snug around him, patrons of Nelson and Nighty. It was said that when Connie was not engaged in a match at Seedhill he would stroll over to the Nighty show behind the sight boards where he appeared to relish the banter against himself and other players. Once, with Nelson in winning vein, Nighty is reported to have said "If tha comes back 'ere next season Connie I don't know who we'se drop for thi." To bowlers taking a long run he said he didn't go as far as that for his holidays.

Nighty's reputation would earn him a place on the wireless. He was a driver for a transport contractor and was interviewed by Victor Smythe of the BBC while "resting" at the Jungle Cafe below Shap Fell. He told of his experiences on the road and of once being snowed up for five days on Shap. Nighty had a cabful of tales, one of a man who acquired a council house and then called at a shop for half a pound of butter. The shopkeeper said if he bought a pound he'd save a halfpenny. "That's awreight but I took a peand hooam last week and couldn't shut t'cupboard door," the customer said.

Constantine, one of the first black men seen around Nelson, would go on to receive the Freedom of the Borough, marking the warmth and respect with which he and his family were held in the town. He would include Nelson in his life peerage title.

As the thirties struggled on and a peace-loving town was jolted into preparing for war its people found relief in sport, concerts, prize-winning choris, cinemas, plays, dancing and performers like Robbie Hayhurst, my spiedon trick rider, who'd been building an international reputation for careering at all angles on a motor bike and was seen and *heard* in the slipstream to hostilities. With copper rods, ball bearings and a gramophone turntable, the *Nelson Leader* reported, he built a model of a ride which was developed full size and gave passengers in small cars on rails the sensation of a motor cyclist on the wall-of-death, in which he specialised.

The daredevil in breeches, belt and leggings, his hair sleeked and tie flying, who I'd seen in practice near home, made his debut as vaudeville artiste with breathtaking feats at the Palace Theatre, feats not attempted on a music hall stage before. His climb up a 9-foot ladder while the bike circled was the climax to a show with the Four Stuarts, brothers in harmony, a ventriloquist, the Nelson Arion Glee Union and Doris Cuban, dancing xylophonist. Malcolm Campbell, no less, called Robbie "the wizard on wheels".

One day the wizard got himself into a little bother and appeared before magistrates for "riding on the highway a motor cycle equipped only for the stage". In a case which would come as light relief a constable said Robbie was riding side-saddle at four miles an hour, feet touching the ground at times. Robbie said he'd wanted it for rehearsals and its transport was being repaired. He was only wheeling it with engine running, leaning on it at times, always trailing his feet and never at more than walking speed. It ran on half a pint of petrol soaked in cotton wool and he'd chosen a quiet road because the bike's red and white colour attracted attention. The magistrates dismissed the case — on payment of 24s costs.

Romany came to town, breathing life into a warm voice from BBC *Children's Hour*. We believed in his walks with dog Raq and felt we were in the countryside with him, "looking" at nature. Little know-alls claimed he was only in the studio, script in hand in front of a microphone, with feverish technicians adding the sounds of horse, sheep and birds. What was more, he was really a Methodist minister though they had to agree that he'd a love of the countryside and his own vardo. As for those plummy-voiced children, we didn't mind that they were really radio aunts Muriel Levy and Doris Campbell. Raq, we understood, was real enough. The Reverend spoke in Nelson when I was twelve to 1,300 mill-town people, drew charcoal sketches and introduced a cocker spaniel called Raq. Whether it was the canine of the broadcasts I never knew. Perhaps the short-trousered cynics were getting to us after all. Nelson had turned a blind eye to government advice on air-raid precautions and anti-gas defences but, as war threatened, changed tack and on the milk round we met air-raid wardens, trenches, siren sites and, by the thousand, those rubber-stink gas masks in brown cardboard boxes — "Place the mask over your head . . . insert your chin first."

Riddles were popular with boys and in May 1938 the town set itself one that may have been easier to solve in the blackness of a Tum Hill night. The idea was to create an absolute blackout in the town early one morning for the pretend follow-up of an air raid. Seven hundred volunteers got up before the cockerels. The only pinpoints of light were from bypass jets in gas lamps and in a setting like a horror film motorists drove eerily on side lights. The only help was from kerbs painted white, but not by a phantom this time. First aid parties in gas masks fumbled around jet-black streets with stretcher cases. More than a hundred wardens, breeding profusely by now it seemed, patrolled their sectors as they waited for the effects of the "raid".

CHAPTER
TWENTY-THREE

The Jesse James Affair

It's no go the merrygoround
It's no go the rickshaw
All we want is a limousine
and a ticket for the peepshow.
Louis MacNeice

In the summer before the balloon went up and we'd long given up the game of cowboys and Indians, Nelson Town Council mustered a posse to run Jesse James out of town. The posse was unarmed but to be fair to the bandit and his skill with the gun he had a distinct handicap. He'd been dead for fifty-seven years.

Contemporary bush telegraph didn't say whether the encounter was at high noon but it was in July 1939 that a deputation of five — two senior police officers, an alderman, town clerk and director of education — moseyed across the cobbled prairies of the town to the annual fair holed up on its recreation ground. By any measurement it was a high-powered posse, and was mustered for a private viewing of a sideshow "Crime Does Not Pay". Its main exhibit was the body of James, US bank and train robber and leader with brother Frank of the Quantrill gang. With a price of $10,000 on his head Jesse had been shot dead by an accomplice in 1882 while hanging a picture in his home.

According to the *Nelson Leader* report his body had been found in the catacombs of Guanjuando in Mexico where the rarefied air had preserved the remains. There was one bullet mark in the forehead and four in the body. The outlaw was in his coffin and draped only in a black loin cloth. The body had been on show in Stretford in Lancashire with no objections to the police. Nelson was being offered the same privilege but some of its people had complained. Mr James White, the showman, told the deputation the body was ossified and bodies were shown in museums without objection. He admitted children because its purpose was to show that crime did not pay. There were bullet holes for them to see what James's fate was.

In a town not unused to the unusual it was, to say the least, bizarre, and Alderman Herbert Throup, chairman of a committee which oddly combined Watch, Parks and Library, stood firm against the outlaw. We were not told whether his back was to the sun. He was against showing the body for profit and there were strong feelings because of the bad taste and sordid appeal of the show. Mr White agreed to replace the show with Prince Amir Ali's Royal Indian Theatre. I was thirteen and didn't patronise the prince, but felt that some boys might have welcomed the one-upmanship of a squint at old Jesse. But then, whatever his crimes, the outlaw deserved better than being trundled through a second notoriety as a peepshow exhibit. Nelson did right not to turn a blind eye towards him.

The travelling fair used to roll up at the close of Wakes Week hopeful that townspeople would have a bob or two left over, and our family would knock off early one evening to see or hear it. We knew it would be on the "rec" but strangers only needed to walk towards the blare which must have knocked a pound or two off the price of nearby houses. Burnley had a pot fair tacked on but ours was all fairground — steam, staging, bright lights, amplified gramophones, sideshows and uneven movement. A straight line was the shortest distance between points but couldn't churn the stomach and the daring looked for more eccentric geometry. It was unusual to circulate far before meeting someone you'd not met since the previous year at the fair which meant ten minutes of mee-mawing under the tin roof, with tugs on mother's coat to move on to the excitement.

"Eee, hasn't she shot up since last year."
"Is that your oldest? Isn't he like his dad?"

"They've buried Frank, you know."
"Eee, is he dead?"

"See yer next year if mi head's on."
"Keep out o't' boxing ring then."

Off on the dusty rounds we wound, then or later, among swingboats, carousels, shooting galleries, switchbacks, hooplas, dodg'ems and spinning rides where young men leapt on with mugs of tea without spilling a drop. I was allowed one or two rides. The caterpillar which wrapped a green skin over us lured courting couples and those who hoped to be. Youths who failed with wooden ball or rifle claimed the coconuts were glued on or the rifle sights were cock-eyed. Dad thought a lot of the stalls were "catchpennies" but would risk rolling a penny or two on the chequered number boards. With sideshows, he said, at least you got "summat for your money".

The boxing booths were not for us. They'd men with puffy eyes and squashed noses in both ring and audience. Dad had been a motor cycle buff so if there was a wall-of-death it would be on our agenda. Riders revved up their machines outside to spark interest. Inside, the bikes crackled close to the danger line, the sectioned woodwork shuddered and we drew back from the parapet of their tube. Death seemed only a mistake away. We queued to see midgets, men and women in tiny clothes and chairs, drinking from miniature cups. Mother thought they were exploited but some felt it was perhaps the only way such little people could earn a living. We had much to learn.

We would watch children leave for home and possibly a "thick ear" for lumbering the house with a prize goldfish in a bowl and we never left the fairground without a bag of chats, small fried potatoes. Spoilsports used to say they'd been washed in the canal. We didn't care. They were tasty, traditional and ended the night on a far from sour note, even when soaked in vinegar.

Summer was for days out. A ramble or car picnic was anticipated all week. Anyone who crossed borders to Scotland or Wales was an explorer. We'd motor to the nearest Yorkshire dale and, once, in a friend's Jowett with umbrella hood, to Flookburgh on Morecambe Bay close to where the last wolf in England was said to have been killed and the isolation tempted Dad's black bathing suit out of hibernation. With time I would begin cycling with friends, sometimes on lanes where the creak of pedals was the only sound. Yellow oilskin capes, pungent and visible, were well used in Lancashire. On one camping expedition the heavy load unbalanced me on a tight lane but thankfully the first motorist to appear was the local doctor, who bandaged my hand.

On another jaunt, to Malham, we camped below Gordale Scar, little changed since visits from John Ruskin, the art critic, Charles Kingsley, the novelist, and William Wordsworth, the poet. We three modest callers were to be noted only and briefly for the fact that one of us tumbled down the scar, with no permanent damage. A shorter run was to Wycoller, hamlet of handloom weaving and farming until cotton lured its workers out, leaving it a ghost village in two senses. A spectral horseman was said to gallop over a bridge there. Its crumbling hall was claimed to have been the Fearndean Manor of *Jane Eyre*. Downstream was Laneshawbridge with its classic eighteenth-century murder. The lover of Hannah Corbridge, it was said,

141

poisoned her with parkin and then cut her throat, and it was claimed that oglers used to travel there to see drops of blood oozing from stones out of the lover's demolished house. Hannah, reputed to have reappeared at times, was exorcised by a priest. As pedal-pushing boys we knew little of these hauntings but would have broken the speed limit if Hannah had shown up. As it was we took our thrills more modestly from pedalling, fresh air and stops for sardine sandwiches and pop.

For wistful travellers with scant means and sound legs the Youth Hostels Association offered cheap digs for small chores. Three of us would in time have the unexpected blush of sharing its Derwent Hall in Derbyshire with hostellers from a Yorkshire girls' school but either they or we must have put a jinx on the place. It would vanish later with a village under a reservoir. While well-heeled youths were going south or getting foreign parts stamped on passports our cards were printed with Endmoor, Coniston, Ingleton and Loughborough and, who knows, we may have been having as much fun and surely more exercise.

Railways took us on summer excursions to the west coast, its posh name, and if pocket money ran to a Nestlé's chocolate bar from a station slot machine so much the sweeter. In hot weather excursionists tumbled from cramped steamy carriages and shoe-horned into cramped steamy spaces on Blackpool beach, and filled everything from socks to sandwiches with sand. You could paddle on floating bread and other unmentionables at the water's edge, or swim out for a mouthful. You could attempt deckchair assembly, lose children, bury dads or slip across the promenade to hoist trivia with a flawed crane in a glass case or peer through binoculars to see what the butler saw, which wasn't much. Children gathered to watch a child strangler beat his wife and arrange a public hanging, a knockabout which had them moist with laughter top and bottom. Punch and Judy was applauded punch by punch.

In Wakes Week the mill workers took holidays together. Many steamed to Blackpool or Morecambe with spare money sewn into vests and those who hoped to avoid a crusty tackler for a day or two could hear his voice from a deckchair on the pier. Some took coach trips, including mystery tours, and others stayed at home to breathe in the unpolluted air of a smokeless town and explore the Victorian parks, Pendleside and its hill, enticing lures like Happy Valley, Palm Beach and Jack Moore's monkey with the creature of the title and, once, a nasty piece of monkey business when some callous human reportedly gave it a lit cigarette. On summer Sundays the parks offered brass band music, from Strauss to Sullivan, and some still remembered an abandoned performance by the Nelson Prize Band when an alderman complained of a broken agreement — it had switched from Victorian classic pieces to a dance tune. The parks would become specially brisk with events for all ages in the holidays-at-homes programme to come in the Second World War, and as that gloomed near the town offered some relief by opening its new open-air swimming pool in Marsden Park. Some thought that in Lancashire such an unroofed affair might be a white elephant. But after thirteen days a thousand souls had paid to go into the pool each day. From his credentials it was certain that Matey would not be among them, though a hint that the pool might become heated could have been tempting.

Two thousand schoolchildren steamed into town from Bradford, evacuees with gas masks and separation tearstains. Reedyford Memorial Hospital began to move patients out against the possible admittance of war casualties.

Peace was slipping out of grasp.

A SECOND DARKNESS

Dad was too old to be called up and I was thirteen on that Sunday in September 1939, when Neville Chamberlain followed a solemn peal of bells on the wireless with the more solemn news that we'd asked Germany to take its troops out of Poland. "I have to tell you now that no such undertaking has been received and that consequently this country is at war with Germany," the Prime Minister intoned.

The news was received in silence and in tears. I understood some of the gravitas of that day from the moist responses of adults who'd been through the first darkness. Dad was eighteen when the Great War ended and had apparently tried to join the Royal Flying Corps by giving a false age. When that out of character deception failed he served with the Lancashire Fusiliers and, as he told it, was detailed to shift courting couples off Flamborough Head on the Yorkshire coast.

As the second darkness fell the wireless set was to be our mouthpiece on the heartache of hostilities. Before the year was out British troops had landed in France, the *Graf Spee* had been scuttled, the warship *Royal Oak* sunk and Myra Hess had started her lunchtime pianoforte recitals. Just before the outbreak our Independent Methodist magazine had shrieked the headline "A National Peril", not the threat of bloodshed but a survey on gambling on football pools. The gamble of war was scarcely touched on, though two months later the magazine reported that the war was reacting "seriously" on the work of churches with darkened streets and the difficulties of travel threatening a witness which was then ever more needed. Lord Haw-Haw with his "Jairmany Calling" broadcasts believed such terms as "honest injun" and "old chap" were in common use here. Careless talk could cost lives and walls had ears.

Gloom lay ahead. There were to be some lighter moments in the British spirit to make the best of things and a boy would be more inclined to reflect on flashes of light in the gloom to come.

CHAPTER
TWENTY-FOUR

Spy Catchers

There never was a good war, or a bad peace.
Benjamin Franklin

With his bombsights on the cities Hermann Goering turned a blind eye to Nelson. Our war was to be indirect. The Germans didn't bomb our chippies but food controllers had to splash out with extra cooking fats to keep them frying. As the town snuffed out its endemic pipe of peace and began to square up to Adolf there was one fragment of the Duration that would evade military historians.

One weekend I was messing about as usual when Dad approached me in the field with a face like a slow handclap. He was flanked, more dwarfed, by two tall men who were a Riot Act on legs. Dad spoke first: "These men would like a word with you," he said with a straight face relieved by a wink. "They'd like to know what you're up to down yonder." He nodded yonder, to a line of hen huts as prosaic and mismatched as a muster of novice Home Guards. "Down yonder, in that hut of yours." There were five or six huts and all except one were his. The exception was mine only because it was henless and more conspicuous. On top of it was an aerial, sticking out like the sore thumb of a bitten postman. That hut was the cause of the deputation. Special Branch, M15 or 6 or just the local constabulary in plain clothes, I never knew which, had come to investigate the mystery of the Little Gib Hill aerial and unmask the spy of Tum Hill who was passing on secrets of our stockpile of catapults and water pistols to the Third Reich. Surely Hitler couldn't have heard of Nelson, still less of Tum Hill. No spy worth his forged passport would leave evidence poked up for all to see. False beards were one thing but even the local bobbies couldn't mistake Dad and me in our braces and black leggings for special agents. We'd nothing to hide, except fear. Luckily, they seemed satisfied with Dad's explanation and grovelling and after good-humoured exchanges about ways of making us talk M15 went on their way. From a distance they looked shorter.

The explanation was simple. Dad allowed me to use the empty cabin as a den, sparsely furnished. For extra cheer, two school friends, do-it-yourself dabblers who probably went on to a Nobel Prize in electronics, had cobbled together a wireless set. Like Matey without pocket money, the set wouldn't work effectively without aerial. Dad, one of the town's 400 wardens still waiting for a red alert on a black telephone, would be pleased to put the affair of the spy catchers behind him. The aerial was taken down to avoid any further hindrance to Mr Churchill's war effort. About the time the Nelson Leader published an advertisement which urged "Kill that rat. It's doing Hitler's Work." I was relieved to find that it was a rat with four legs, though probably not one of ours.

Newspapers and the BBC were reporting that shops across the nation were selling out of blackout material for curtains. Mother, the magic improviser, probably made ours out of "something put by". Even a chink up there could wink at Goering's Luftwaffe but the only air raid warden around was Dad and as he was assigned to a post in the upper part of town he may not have had authority over us.

From her armchair scrutiny of the local paper Mother offered us snippets on Nelson's war blackout: the first pedestrian knocked down in it, people with "blackout nerves", a second-hand dealer booked for blackout offences, then the first poignant intrusion of the darkness beyond — the reported death of a young marine, the start of a pattern of telegram boys on doorsteps with news of men killed, missing or taken prisoner. From the box on the sideboard a breezy Handley and mumbling Wilton joked long to light up our darkness, and if the Führer had invaded during *ITMA* (*It's That Man Again*) he could have caught us napping, with Fumf speaking to some 16 million in a week.

We entertained *ourselves* too. Many homes aspired to an upright piano for upright home music and so eventually would ours. For lessons I was wished on a small gentle lady who had done us no harm. After six months something interrupted my lessons, possibly too many "Bluebells of Scotland" in Dad's ears. The piano became a repository for ornaments on top, and letters under the lid. I had learned enough to play popular tunes by ear, allowing for faulty left-hand fingering, and would much later be recruited for background tinkling at someone's wedding reception where wrong notes would be concealed in the celebrating and the intoning by the bride's father of the one-eyed yellow idol to the north of Katmandu.

Any chapel-going family was immersed in music in some way but there was to be one musical feast that would be memorable for me. Mother announced that for a treat she'd take me to hear *Madame Butterfly*. "Who's she?" I wondered. I'd seen madams in concert at the chapel and butterflies on nettles behind the pigsty but never the two together. There were women on Blackpool's Golden Mile who called themselves madam. They told fortunes but mother didn't believe in black magic. I would just have to wait.

When treating day came we took a bus to Burnley. Not much of a treat, a bus ride, even on the top deck. We arrived at the theatre and from its posters it was obvious foreigners were involved. "We're going to see opera," Mother announced grandly. Opera? We climbed up and up and up almost to the roof. Perhaps opera was a star but it was still daylight outside. We sat down in the ceiling with a bird's-eye view of a circle which was only half a circle and some stalls that were nothing like where Dad wintered his cows. It was all new and puzzling. "That's the pit where the orchestra play." Were they miners then? I knew Burnley had mines. The orchestra filed in and began to play fancy music and when the curtains opened I'd heard or seen nothing like it. The stage was huge and we were in Japan. The voices were huge, too, and the sounds coming out different from any Sunday school chorus I'd known, sort of drawn out to fit the movements of the singers, sometimes high and sometimes low and sad, especially where Madame Butterfly kills herself, though no blood or anything. And we looked down on it all from that great height. Later I was told that ours, the cheapest seats, were known as the "gods" and I suppose we were a bit godlike up there. "You've had a bit of culture then?"

Outside again the gloom of evening and of war was being faced. Within a month of Mr Churchill becoming Prime Minister a tattered army had been shipped out of Dunkirk. One British officer had shot a German motor cyclist to splutter to Dunkirk on the Führer's petrol. "They're all somebody's lads," Mother would say, with sympathy for women on both sides which only mothers could feel.

CHAPTER
TWENTY-FIVE

A Funny Thing Happened...

Tickle and entertain us or we die.
William Cowper

Mid-winter. Rain polished pavements as we sloshed into the warmth, handed in damp tickets and settled into shows by "young" men, plays by the ladies' class and imported entertainment by the Merrymakers and other concert parties. Nose-blowing, the rustle of gossip and toffee bags and children on the front row, an audience in from a week's work and school and a wet night saying "Go on then, make us laugh."

Much of the entertaining at Salem Chapel "do's" was homegrown but the concert parties had found their niche with us as in many church halls and Co-op rooms across the north, unwrapping themselves from taxis from somewhere in Lancashire or across the moors in Yorkshire. Our annual compact with the concert party was the "At Homes" with children watching every twitch of the blue and gold stage curtains, hoping that the official opener wouldn't take too long over the "few words". Then the curtains slid back. It was on. The pianist jerked into action. The notes bounced down. The entertainers, five or six

151

abreast, chirpy as chaffinches, jollied out their long helloooooo.

> Here we are again
> Happy as can be
> All good friends
> And jolly good companee.

The concert party would normally have tenor, baritone (or bass), soprano, contralto, comic and pianist. Sometimes the quaint word soubrette appeared and at least one group had a child impersonator. Earlier parties had been the Viennese, the Dominant and the Uppergreen Five, "dispellers of depression", and the Savoy, Grosvenor and Merrymakers were current. Rousing opening choruses were standard and aimed to unwind workers who'd been tied to six looms all week. Solos, duets and quartets were spiced with stand-up comedy and sketches. We loved the silly bits but the search for "The Lost Chord" would drag on. Parties travelled light with a change of clothes for the finale. Props were simple and often borrowed from the host. One minute a tenor would be offering the "keys of heaven" to an ample soprano and the next a table would be placed centre stage for anything from doctor's surgery to classroom. The tenor could appear in white coat as doctor, the soprano as patient with interruptions from the comic who'd called to say he'd "getten't gravel". At his fourth interruption the doctor would erupt and tell the man to wait his turn. "But doctor," he'd protest, "I've getten't gravel. Two tons of it int' waggin outside and I'm blocking t' lane. Where does ter want it tipped?"

The adults laughed, at least the first time, and explained it to the children. We all joined in the applause whether understood or not in the goodwill of an event in which dads dug hard-earned coppers out of pockets for pop and treats and the whole was topped off with a hot supper. It was a "right good night out". People didn't ask for much.

The chapel's Young Men's Fellowship was organised from a basement with two full-sized billiard tables and a table tennis table and had committees on everything from sport to education. One of its last lectures of the Duration would be by a Dr Culbert on "The Economic Development of the USSR" and was probably arranged by the young-at-heart Cyril Robinson, bank manager, fell walker and preacher, who ran debates across the billiard tables and scribbled his minutes down on the back of an envelope retrieved from an inside pocket.

The Fellowship organised dances and shows with rehearsals dovetailed into homework, sport and, for some, courting. By some miracle, though how many believed in miracles was not known, the shows pulled in big audiences and "came off" with a few fluffs and occasional squinting at unsure lines pinned on to the back of the fellow in front. And always with the YMF the unexpected. For one fancy dress event one member would have himself delivered as a parcel. All that and, ultimately, a Pistol Packers' band bouncing out Woodchoppers' Ball and other swing numbers.

Once a year members of the ladies' class would appear bewhiskered and moustachioed in borrowed men's jackets and trousers for the ladies' class play. One wartime Christmas Eve social provided broth for supper made with sheep's head complete, as one spoilsport put it, with its brains — though those who'd seen sheep jumping over imaginary fences had doubts about the brains.

Ultimately in Sunday School we were in the Sabbath care of Mr Taylor, a benign headmaster, who supervised the Intermediates and shepherded his flock on carolling expeditions on crisp December evenings without losing one of them. He used to rap or ring at the doors of church members and then tap his tuning fork on the door jamb to handicap us for the starting note. By then the doorstep audience was in place and we'd be well launched on "O come all ye faithful", heartened that the faithful would come to stand in the cold air to hear us. We encored, perhaps on "While shepherds watched . . ." with, who knows, one or two washing their socks at the back of the group. Afterwards we'd thaw out on Mrs Taylor's pie and peas.

Fading from memory almost by now was one uphill struggle for front-row-fidgeters when a Miss Ainsworth, Gold Medallist, and her dramatic class presented the following bill:

The Newsboy's Debt (recital)
Blatherwick's Diplomacy (drawing-room farce)
Uncle Ben (play)

154

Scenes from *Macbeth* (Shakespeare)
Maggie's Dilemma (comedy)

I expect toffee would see us through the bankrupt newsboy and pop through Blatherwick's blathering but halfway through *Uncle Ben* patience would unravel and come apart in that Scottish play. As for poor Maggie, her dilemma would have no attention. At a guess, and from a distance, that must have been the most trying night of the winter for children, if not of the childhood.

CHAPTER
TWENTY-SIX

An Affair with Marge

I never expect a soldier to think.
George Bernard Shaw

A Sabbath morning in early autumn. The trees were parachuting first bronzed leaves. The breakfast eggs were powdered. Someone, somewhere, was preaching from the Sermon on the Mount — "blessed are the peacemakers". Gunfire was ricocheting from stone walls but its bark was worse than its bite. The seventh day was being trespassed by the blank ammunition of the Pendle Forest companies of the Home Guard who'd been ordered to invade Burnley, our substantial neighbour. The exercise would include what I could only call "the affair of the margarine missile".

As the rural attack advanced on the outskirts of Burnley one of its young invaders felt obliged to slip into someone's house to hide from the defenders. Inside, he met a battle scene that had nothing to do with the war and would never appear in the annals of military history. The lady of the house picked up a slab of margarine and hurled it at her husband's head, to miss her target, as she put it, "for this morning", with a hint that she may have lost the battle

156

but not the war. The marge, intended to add a little colour to wartime bread, spread itself on a wall mirror instead. The Home Guard did not delay to watch the marge wiped off for its prescribed use but slunk away from the private war zone to collide with his own enemy, waiting patiently to demand his surrender. Ambushed, if you like, by half a pound of wartime marge.

Caught off guard as war began, the unpaid domestic army had been mustering across the nation with museum cutlasses, shotguns, spears, catapults and broomsticks made fierce with carving knives. Some had armed themselves with piano wire to booby-trap lanes and behead motor cyclists, theirs, not ours. One Lancashire unit, at least, had orders not to cross its boundary to seize a German pilot if one should bale out. Imagine the questioning if one of our Home Guards had pottered up with a German at the sharp end of his broomstick and that boundary rule had been observed:

Sergeant:	Where did he come from?
Private:	T'other side o' Bott Lane, Sarge. Hanging on his chute from a big sycamore tree.
Sergeant:	Bott Lane, lad. That's Colne, near enough, in'it? Outside our patch. You'll just have to tek him back again and look for one of their lot. Hang 'im back up for t'time being if they're out. What's that? Can 'e have his dinner first? Bloomin' cheek.

★ ★ ★

With time, weapons improved and on a Tuesday evening Nelson found itself under siege to test battlecraft in streets. Home Guards had been "dropped" as German paratroops in Noggarth, White Walls and Catlow Bottoms. Defenders held out late supported by thunder flashes, blank ammunition and cracker blank. After one such engagement of the time an observer said the men could never be perfect as there were no bombs or bullets to put them, and their enthusiasm, out of action. They just wouldn't lie down, he said — a complaint not unknown to us boys from our games of cowboys and Indians.

Our Home Guards had no call for street maps or fingerposts to point them towards "enemy" targets but strangers must have found their absence a problem. Nelson, a relatively young town, lacked the quaint names of older communities though Bacon and Fry Streets taken together, and Causey Foot on its own, could offer a moment's spice on a wet wartime Monday morning. Imagine the reaction of any ejected German pilot consulting a map with some of the names around us — Seghole, Wackersall, Hencock, Ouzle Rock, Lumb Spout.

In one local Home Guard exercise flags were used to represent gunfire. A commander would step out and flag the direction of fire, though whether the flag had *bang* on it was not recorded. For all that, the British managed to halt the Germans in Regent Street, Forest Street and Raikes House Road by which time the Home Guards would be flagging in the other sense and the spam sandwiches long eaten. They gave of their best

158

in the cause and respected their own. A corporal boot and shoe repairer who died naturally was given full military honours at the cemetery. All the training went on and on but mercifully for us without contact with the real enemy.

Wardens like Dad drew various reactions as they offered what advice they could on water buckets, sand and window protection and snooped for chinks of light. Even men lighting cigarettes could be heckled to "Put that light out". As boys practised "In the Mood" as a piano party piece the town was coping with petrol queues, rationing, daylight-only weaving in mills, and among its spread of air-raid shelters was one adapted for the purpose in our own Sunday School basement.

First casualties from air raids in the north-west had been two budgerigars in Liverpool. The real terror had followed with devastating raids on Manchester and Liverpool and then towns and cities to the east of us. Bombers droning overhead in the dead of night would prompt the nervous question "Is it one of ours or one of theirs?" Somehow the drone of ours and theirs was different and boys reckoned to have fathomed out the difference.

Humour again spiced all and the drumming of aeroplane engines triggered perhaps the frailest joke of the Duration. No, not that one, sergeant major! The one where the wife takes an aircraft overhead to be the Luftwaffe.

"Gerry's o'er," she calls out to her sleepier half.
"Don't worry, luv. We'll mop it up in t'morning."

★ ★ ★

Whether the joke survived as long as the chamber-pots on which it was based we never heard.

It had been September 1940 when Nelson had its first genuine alert. Many people stayed indoors. Some hurried into shelters. No bombs fell. None dropped on the town throughout the war, though some people crossed into Colne to see a crater left by one on a hillside near Fox Clough, close to where some eighty years before my great-grandfather's soul had "flamed with light" and changed his life on his knees in that farm outbuilding. The stray bomb was possibly jettisoned by a pilot to lighten his load on his way home to the Fatherland and thankfully left no casualty behind. We had much blessing from being non-strategic — but the blackout was the setting for a callous murder for which we could not otherwise blame the Third Reich.

CHAPTER
TWENTY-SEVEN

Girl in the Blackout

*... but men loved darkness instead of light because
their deeds were evil.*

John 3, 19

The last stop on the train as it wheezed below Tum Hill
towards Yorkshire was the ancient town of Colne, which
climbed stiffly uphill from three sides. Its main street
rose to a Norman church and the town had stocks for
three offenders at once, its own song "Bonnie Colne on
the Hill" and a memorial to Wallace Hartley, conductor
of the band on the *Titanic*. The town, like all of us, was
in the grip of the blackout on a wet night in March
when a girl of nineteen was stabbed at a bus stop below
the church. The police called it "one of the worst
blackout nights". Against the bleak toll from hostilities
the murder of Eileen Barrett was a cowardly, local and
apparently pointless outrage which touched every
family in the community and beyond.

Eileen left home in Trawden for a dressmaking class
at the Colne Technical College to finish a dress in the
last class before examination. After class she was
waiting at a bus stop in the blacked-out Linden Road
when a man loomed out of the night, put an arm round

161

her neck and seized her by the throat. She felt something pierce her back but didn't realise she'd been stabbed. As the gloom masked her attacker two men heard her screams. They were taking the same bus and travelled with her to a bus station on the boundary of Colne and Trawden. As one of them helped her from the bus he noticed blood. Eileen died later in hospital.

As Trawden mourned the loss some were questioning a possible link between her death and an attack by a man on a servant girl on the Burnley side of the Nelson boundary. This girl, out walking, managed to free herself and escape. The Nelson Leader said the incident "lent colour to the suggestion that Miss Barrett's murder was the work of a maniac". No murderer, maniac or otherwise, could be traced. Within three months the police had taken statements from 574 people and another 5,000 had been interviewed without statement. Two hundred guests from a Cooperative Society dance and whist drive that fatal night were traced and interviewed. At length, the police admitted they hadn't a single clue on which to work and the murder in the blackout remained in their files as unsolved.

Meanwhile the military death toll was going on and on with ITMA, Billy Cotton and Workers' Playtime punctuating the grave bulletins from the Front. Rationing by points and clothes by coupon, even down to one for a tie, had in theory imposed equality of sacrifice though I, for one, would happily have sacrificed my soap ration. Food facts were on offer from the bakelite face on the farmhouse dresser but how much the meals on its square scrubbed table were based on them was not noted by a boy. Rumours reached us of egg-smuggling and under-the-counter deals and one gem from Yorkshire of a coffin spirited down from a farm with due respect for the deceased, a black market pig. Some reports were authentic, others more doubtful but in the cold climate of war all were absorbed with some relief. There were gestures. One woman was shopping at a bakery when she met another with six hungry sons to feed, and gave up some of her ration.

Farmers were urged to dig for victory but Tum Hill probably grew nothing more than grass, blackberries and nettles for beer. On the van's travels posters were urging the public to save, shun travel and waste and not to spread rumours. Breathing was allowed but not easily in gas mask practices. Newspaper boys whistled tunes about runaway rabbits, rats in quartermasters' stores, a London nightingale and even whispering grass. Women were advised to save wood by wearing flatter heels though our family didn't go high on theirs. Of more interest to boys were gas buses which zeppelined past the milk van on one route, refilling rooftop bags with town gas from machines like petrol pumps. Tethered inflatables above city rooftops inspired one children's writer to offer Boo Boo the Barrage Balloon for bedtime reading.

Princess Elizabeth broadcast to evacuees and some of ours began to drift back to Bradford but not for that reason. We'd also absorbed some from Manchester and from the south. One southerner was disappointed to find that while many Nelson women wore clogs not many had shawls and she'd seen the two as a natural combination. Too much of Gracie Fields perhaps!

In the second winter of war, church services, dances, concerts and plays in churches helped to cushion depression. Victor Silvester's strict tempo with muted violin, clarinet and alto sax oozed out of gramophones as youths with free-range acne and girls with eyebrow-pencilled seams flirted with the quickstep and with each other. A box in the entrance to our chapel invited money for comforts for serving members and Madame Marianne Mislap-Kapper, Viennese mezzo-soprano and alliterative mouthful, was booked to raise money for the Friends' War Relief Service. Our upper concert room became a Sunday night haunt for young people drawn like moths off the jet-black streets for films which varied from moral stories to nature documentaries. The chapel's deacon of repairs built himself a wooden projection box and almost seemed to hibernate in it.

Iron railings were called up and a defendant in court raised a smile when he mentioned the banana room of his warehouse. The Bench were trying to remember what a banana looked like. Others may have smiled when they saw the town hall steps being painted again, officially now with silver to help us in the blackout. Cotton was losing workers to ammunition factories and itself working on war fabrics. School assemblies were muffled to hear of Old Boys sacrificed for the cause. Our history master turned RAF corporal, Mr Beeston, was on the *Ack-Ack Beer-Beer* programme on the wireless, "a change for him", as a supporter said, "from making the 1832 Reform Bill sound interesting". As 1942 wearied to a close we were freed at least from the gas mask except in "special circumstances" but, less happily, some children in town had taken to lighting balls of paper wrapped around old celluloid films and posting them as imitation bombs through letter-boxes. They were thought to be copying guerrilla fighters behind German lines in Russia.

Two pigeons had "adopted" us at the hillside, more pets than potential. With time we'd realise that pigeon fanciers had been earning twopence for every bird that flew for an Army Pigeon Service. Birds were dropped over enemy-occupied territory with questionnaires attached, and thirty-two got medals for gallantry. Our pair would probably have turned back for their corn.

Churchill's riposte to Hitler was chicken-based. "Some chicken, some neck," he growled to Adolf's claim that in three weeks England's neck would have been wrung like a chicken's. We knew a little about chickens and, sadly for me, about the wringing of their necks at Tum Hill but we were about to desert all three, chickens, neck-wringing and the hill itself, and move out of the draught.

CHAPTER
TWENTY-EIGHT

Townie

In the middle of the war Dad gave up the farm and we settled in town, a house with an attic in a terraced row outside a small triangular park lost largely to air-raid shelters. There was a chip shop near the top of the terrace and a Cooperative store down the road, though we didn't take up offers of the "divi". Time would erase the farm sale but I often imagined my parents' heartache as a family jigsaw came apart under an auctioneer's hammer, reviving for Mother the image of a father who stood on carts at farm sales shouting up the prices of sheep and cows and buckets and carts and food hoppers. In years to come I'd see farmers creaking like sheds and looking for a just nest-egg for retirement from a lifetime's work. It hadn't been anything like a lifetime for Mother and Dad but the wrench would still be felt.

Apart from the bonus of being able to smell the opening of doors at the chip shop and collect a family meal wrapped in newspaper without bicycle there was one further consolation from being town-based. I no longer had to sneak past the area where the shortest bully lived. Although by then I'd cultivated enough tall mates and tall stories to keep the threats under control and we were all "growing up", the ghost of the shortest still haunted me as I passed by.

By then too I was absorbed in homework, Sunday School and cycling but the changeover from field to street was at least naturally and geographically strange to me. One handed-down snap would show a few of us attempting cricket, yes cricket for Matey, on that rough plot shared with air-raid shelters, thankfully unused. The walk from there to school took in cobbled streets and a ginnel between mills, grey against the green of paths from the farm. Mornings meant hurried dashes to school but some of the schoolbag and ink-fingered saunters home were spiced by the adolescent "chase", not mine but that of an athletic friend with me who was pursuing a young lady. Pursuit had reached the trailing, hailing and cap-setting stage and the pursued and her companion were at risk of retort neck from turning to hurl arrows of pretend indifference. In such flirting rituals the human cuts an absurd figure for despite a "get lost" air the girl was already two-thirds and a bit won over. Such chatting-up garnishes in class, corridor or road home made algebra seem almost tolerable. Without the educational system the human race may well have faded out.

We'd graduated by age in school to an annual dance which in a place of learning felt obliged to advertise itself as a soirée and had sent some of us early on to our dictionaries to see whether it meant something boring or offered anything to eat. Patently, it was to underline the difference. We had to partner girls and rehearse various dances before the real test. Even so, as one with faulty signalling from brain to feet, I'd been concerned that my partner would survive the dances without injury. By coincidence I was partnered by a milkman's daughter though we would not pass much time discussing the price of milk. More likely, the price of a new pair of dance shoes (hers). I don't think she was hobbling the morning after. I may have been, of course.

In our closing months at the school some of us exchanged entries in autograph albums. That year I'd "inherited" Dad's album with its pastel-coloured pages, written my name and V Upper Q in its front and began to canvass entries. The album already had a few from Dad's boyhood including a poem by Ella Wheeler Wilcox — "I know not whence I came/I know not whither I go" — which suggested a chronic lack of signposting.

Girls' albums were peppered with rhymes, sketches of ladies and flowers and turned-up corners with dark secrets marked "For men only" (underpants) and "For women only" (corsets). Any book belonging to boy or girl that "chanced to roam" risked having its ears boxed. Three girls only worked on my album — two with sketches of girls in profile with hairstyles of the time and the third, more daringly, a girl in negligée and suspenders (untitled). The remainder was male and obviously so — aircraft of the period, the inevitable wartime cartoons, one on the Home Guard and another on a Japanese theme. The last page was not hooked or crooked but showed the inner workings of a wireless set captioned "The piece that passeth all understanding". Two Burgess brothers with whom I enjoyed cycle outings left evocations of the countryside, and the chalk eater a sketch of a Disney-like character running away from work. At a guess the following were probably common to many albums:

> In a parlour there were three
> A maid, a parlour lamp and he
> Two's company without a doubt
> And so the parlour lamp went out.

> Two in a hammock attempted to kiss
> When all of a sudden they landed
> like this!

Back in the town Dad returned to the precise thous' of his trade as a turner in an engineering shop. Perhaps I missed the stillness of the farm for doing homework because as School Certificate loomed I was school-bagged off to stay with cousin Doris in the quietness of Sabden Fold and with my back to a stone wall got down to my studies. After the examination work would be calling, not for pocket money for pictures or new cycle clips, but for a living.

Against the trauma of war and its impact on some of our serving staff members and former students we would remember some of the lighter moments of our school days which were disciplined but fair and academically stimulating. My fond memories of the school were not all associated with how much profit I put into Wall's ice-cream through their tricycle man at

169

the gates. It had to end. University was for the few and most of us were to leave school to pick up what threads we could from the college of life in a cotton town.

CHAPTER
TWENTY-NINE

On the Pink

*. . . and where roads and newspapers lay
everything open.*

Jane Austen

As if school and Sunday School were not enough
learning, some of us blind-man's buffed our way
through the blackout in the early forties to discover
night school. I found myself in a shorthand class
fragrant with potential secretaries. If there was one
other male there his name eludes me. Shorthand wasn't
normally demanded for male careers but essential to
the one I was to follow. A classful of girls transmitting
a morse code of "Californian Poppy" or "Evening
in Paris" guaranteed a message received from a
seventeen-year-old with red hair and a novel pimple
every week. Isaac Pitman's curves in the primer had
competition. To make matters more blushing the typing
class, also essential, was otherwise all-female. We typed
there to jaunty tunes with typewriter bells going off
wildly and quick brown foxes scampering over lazy
dogs as if the Pendle Forest Hunt was in pink pursuit.
Ultimately I left that school-of-the-night with one out
of two, failure in typing, success in shorthand. I could

have blamed the failure, ungallantly, on some twenty or so distractions but put it down to the fact that my typing paper slipped halfway through the test.

I never could remember the tunes.

I'd opted for journalism as a career and needed shorthand and typing skills before being let loose on the news potential of the industrious people of Nelson and Colne. Newspaper work came up almost by chance. After I applied to Mr Donald Race, solicitor, without success and escaped the lucrative treadmill of the law, Uncle Wilson, newsagent, saw my school report and said it suggested journalism. As he sold newspapers I considered him qualified to pronounce, especially when School Certificate results confirmed a bias towards English and languages. I tried for a reporter's job. "You're going to work for't Pink. You'll need a trilby, lad," someone advised. Though he didn't mention a press card on its brim I thought he'd seen too many hold-the-front-page movies from the US of A.

The *Northern Daily Telegraph*, chummily called the Pink because its Saturday sports edition was on pink paper, was the evening newspaper for the region with head office in Blackburn. It had served the community long enough to have a pigeon loft in its tower to which homing pigeons used to flap home with football scores. For all my feathered credentials I was relieved that was a mail system that time and telephones had put to flight. I had to report to Frank Sim, a gentle Manxman and Methodist local preacher, who was to initiate me into the profession. Mr Sim, a district reporter, occupied the first floor of a branch office in Manchester

Road, Nelson, with bus parcel office, Yorkshire Penny Bank, an optician's and a public urinal as near neighbours. Towards teatime on each working day we would compete with a raucous "bush" machine gabbling away on the ground floor. It stamped the latest racing results into the fudge (stop press column) of the papers as they arrived by breathless pink van from Blackburn, giving local punters the tip to sing or cry into their beers. The papers were then reparcelled under named wrappers and hurried on to buses for newsagents and to the seller shouting *Telegraph* or something like it in the town centre. Street sellers had managed to avoid elocution lessons and aimed for the most convoluted cries to sell their news. One, in another town, must have learned to shout with his fingers trapped in a door and it was safer to glance at the contents board for the headline of the night. The Nelson vendor stood at the junction of Manchester Road, Leeds Road and Scotland Road. If anyone asked directions he could set them off in roughly the right direction for Leeds or Manchester but his directions for Scotland would have been worth hearing.

Junior reporter. That was the designation and as a condition of learning to write reports I had to clean windows. I didn't mind making coffee because the machine men below taught how a pinch of salt enhanced the taste and that wrinkle, if no other, stayed with me. So, with two-thirds of the war behind I set out with Pitman notebook and HB pencils to jot down the happenings, major, middling and mediocre to two boroughs, three urban districts and a pottering of

173

villages answering to a rural district council. Most of it would prove to be middling. I hung my gaberdine raincoat next to the chief's behind the door in that upper room and felt to have arrived. In time, a trilby found itself on the same hook. Red-rose-rain called for a lid on the head.

Frank Sim's upper room held a long solid desk with telephone, copy paper, diary and two typewriters of a kind and weight that must have doubled the hernia list at the local hospital. His desk drawer concealed a novel of fading sheets which, to my knowledge, never gave itself up. Its author was a bald, mild-mannered man with spectacles, a reporter of long pencilling and a committed Christian with a cantering unease about how his copy would be handled or mishandled by the sub-editors in Blackburn. "I never read our paper until I've had my tea," he used to say as he waited for calls from copy girls to take down his reports over the telephone.

He'd long served as a local preacher and class speaker but a similar threat to his digestion would lie in wait in the men's class of my own chapel which had nurtured politicians. Debates followed talks at times, with challenges from one man in particular. "I'm in the lion's den on Sunday. Will you-know-who be there?" You-know-who would surely be there and a Monday morning inquest would be held on a Daniel thrown to the lion. He never shirked it, though, my honourable tutor, and I came to respect both man and advice. Back he would come from the magistrates' court to a mutual plugging of gaps in shorthand with tubby reporter Billy

Bury, of the *Burnley Express*, who chirpily covered the same patch and had sergeant-majored an officeful of clerks in the Great War.

Junior reporters were weaned on fires that didn't quite get going, bumps that didn't quite maim, talks that didn't matter much, deaths of people who hadn't made their mark and lighthearted fillers. Weddings were on their agenda and the golden and diamond celebrations of them. "Will it be in't Pink then?" a diamond wedding pair would ask after pagefuls of notes had been taken down. "Shouldn't 'e 'ave 'is collar on for t'picture. Shouldn't he get out of them pants 'e paints in. Oh, I see. It'll only be t'top half. No need to bother, 'e sez. But tek that old cap off. I've threatened to put it in t'bin."

Deaths were reported with as much sympathy as possible. At times I was asked if I would like to go through and see the beloved, as if doubting demise. In one hushed parlour I was interviewing a widow when the undertaker arrived to collect the loved one from a bedroom. "Can you give us a hand?" he said. "Only it's an awkward staircase and we're short-handed." He didn't mention that the deceased was heavy. Care had to be taken to make sure that deaths were not reported prematurely. In one district a man at the front counter was anxious to say that, contrary to that evening's edition, he had not died. A reporter with some tact persuaded him to go on his way counting his blessings. Hoaxing could be a risk. Perhaps as a warning I was told that one reporter had accepted information that the stationmaster of Sabden had died. Luckily, someone knew that Sabden was not on the railway. The social pecking order was conspicuous even in death. For those warranting big headlines the names of mourners were scribbled down at the graveyard gate. It could be a chill stint in a stiff wind threatening ageing reporters with a return to those very gates after pneumonia.

We kept contacts and personal or telephone links with the emergency services and at set intervals with political agents, clergy and council committee clerks. Thoroughness was the backbone of journalism and that disciplined contact would pay off in years to come when an alderman at an art exhibition discreetly advised me to look at the town hall notice-board. The mayor, a pacifist, had resigned because the guard of honour for a royal visit would be carrying rifles. It would be an international exclusive.

Our main rivals were the weekly newspapers which printed a minutiae of local movement, a bound record for historians. In theory we had six days to scoop them but they would sometimes explode a bombshell on the seventh. Overnight reports on council meetings and elections had to be typed up and in a train envelope on a guards van to Blackburn before the town was stirring. One night I was typing in the upper room after the town's bedtime, with the street below as empty as a prisoner's diary, a silence eerie in itself. Suddenly I heard heavy footsteps on the wooden stairs which matched my heartbeats in timing. Nearernearernearer. The door was flung open. A boot appeared.

"Thought you were a burglar," the policeman said. "Shouldn't leave the door unlocked, you know."

Policemen checked door handles in the town centre and ours had been found wanting. I couldn't quite accept that a burglar would have been nicking with all the lights on.

The fast and deadline work had to be leavened by humour. Frank Sim once left his trilby upturned on a table at the back of a trades union meeting and the brothers, assuming it was for the collection, flung hard-earned coins into it. Once, my chief accidentally took off to court in my raincoat, like his own but more geriatric. After court he inspected the coat on its hook, disowned it and returned coatless. Back in the court corridor to retrieve the shabby garment I hoped I wouldn't be suspected of pinching my own coat.

Cuthbert Colling, at the Blackburn end of the telephone, was a news editor who blew from genial to brusque but was generally fair with it. The newspaper would eventually have two features for which reporters were expected to write items — "Table Talk", a gossipy column, and "Over the Teacups", for women readers. As an offshoot from his news editing Mr Colling had made himself a geologist in search of these gems and it was worth supplying the items if only to bathe in his gruff gratitude.

CHAPTER
THIRTY

Another Upper Room

Bert Shackleton was an affable pipe-smoking ex-guardsman with drill square shoulders who'd served in the Kaiser's war. He was the *Telegraph*'s chief reporter in Burnley, our bigger neighbour, and I was transferred there for continuing training. Burnley reporters were also destined for an upper room above reception, advertising and the sounds of the street below. We would type our reports, three reporters at a square table, again prompting a question — what would the British newspaper industry have done without the products of upper rooms?

The chief occupied a swivel-chair and in a drift of smoke swivelled to assign jobs from a diary on a rolled-top desk which he rolled and unrolled and kept, like his notebooks, with military neatness and precision. He had a brisk attachment to sport and doubled as Watchman, his pseudonym for dispatches from Burnley matches, the Clarets, and cricket in the Lancashire League locally. I never met anyone who spoke ill of Bert Shackleton, even though at times newsmen have to "put down" their subjects. Like Frank Sim, he was one of those gentlemen of the press whose word was their bond, fair almost to a fault and careful to protect his sources.

The chief's shorthand and handwriting could have come from a textbook and he had taught shorthand. One of my duties was to run, not quite literally, his reports from Turf Moor football ground to a power point underneath the stand for a plug-in portable telephone. Watchman wrote on pages divided into spaces, one word per space and so many words to the page, so that he could calculate his share of the Sports Pink. I never remember questioning one word, which was unlike the story of one news editor's scribble whose writing was a daily crossword puzzle to the compositors. Rumour had it that they became so adept at transcription that a chicken with inky feet was allowed to walk across a page and the squiggle sent down to the composing room. After some time one of the comps emerged with the page and a polite request. "We can get most of this, sir, but there's just this one word here we can't make out." A likely story.

The local music and drama festivals were cultural threads in the fabric of mill towns with a long tradition in those skills, especially in churches and chapels. In their time reporters would cover such events. For me, the scribe, the one-act play festivals were business with pleasure but "Hark, Hark, the Lark" thirteen times or twenty-five "Water Wagtails" on the pianoforte were too much like being kept in to write lines. We left that marathon to the adjudicators, some of whom lived up to their long and fancy names by speaking at length and spicing their criticisms with sarcasm at the expense of humbled entrants. Result-taking was a bore for wordsmiths who preferred story writing to league tables. School speech days were tolerable, perhaps because we were no longer a uniformed target immobilised through windbagging. But there was no consoling day's holiday for the reporter.

Contacts, again, were vital. Our tip-offs for the urban district of Padiham, for example, centred on a man who sounded military and had the moustache for it. Major Hargreaves, short, broad, bespectacled, had a thorough grasp of the little town, was its Weavers' Secretary and a councillor who happened to have been given Major as a first name.

Among diary duties for reporters in Burnley was the noting down of a hospital bulletin, a code system published each day on the condition of patients in an isolation hospital. Progress or otherwise was coded in categories known only to relatives and a mistake could devastate a family. Bulletin girls and reporters remained unseen at opposite ends of a telephone line and I arranged to see one of the girls. No romance followed. Similarly, almost, I negotiated a rendezvous with a girl of telephone acquaintance in another town whom I'd seen only once. As the train steamed towards her whistling at mill chimneys and canal barges I couldn't remember her face, and she probably couldn't remember mine. Powdered faces on dim stations gave no hint of hers, and I began to wish I'd done a Ronald Colman and worn a red rose. Poor girl. It would have been too much — red hair, red rose, red nose. Her turn for the distress signal. We did find each other in our neutral town and went off to the pictures. I couldn't remember the film. No romance followed. The telephone was proving to be no way to a girl's heart.

Sometimes our profession would print out a reporter who was larger than the average life, more like an actor's portrayal of a journalist. One such hale and hearty scribe signalled arrival as if megaphoning to a strike meeting, almost always good-humoured. Perhaps on our lowly returns we envied him a little when he pulled unopened wage packets out of an inside pocket. He was likeable enough if you could withstand avalanches and with only basic courage myself I would have shadowed him bravely into any menacing engagement.

In contrast, another reporter from a rival evening newspaper would haunt the town, hurrying from one assignment to the next and appreciating the help of competitors because he was a one-man operation expected to magpie the choicest news from each day. Arriving from court on some other news scene, breathless with cigarette ash snowing to notepad, he'd say "Not much in it, is there? I only want a par!" A paragraph was all time and space would allow on most topics and, notebook Pitmanned with pars, he'd retire to his telephone and give his paper a summary of events, go home and prepare for the next unequal fag-ash and foraging day.

One of our aids to the war effort in Burnley was to take turns on a camp bed overnight for firewatching. Nothing more alarming than pipefuls of Erinmore tobacco or Player's cigarettes caught fire and the only discovery was of a bank clerk firewatcher asleep on the communal camp bed when we blearied in for work. Much of the war news with a north-west slant, bombs on cities apart, was happening to "our lads" in the Forces, though elsewhere in Lancashire journalists were reporting on prisoners of war and escape attempts without benefit of wooden horses. Seven took off from a mill prison in Oldham, all rounded up, one by a girl porter at a Derbyshire railway station. Our Independent Methodist magazine reported in 1942 that one of our churches in Wigan and one in Liverpool had been wrecked by bombs, and our minds had been absorbing from the wireless far-away places wrenched into prominence by simply lying in the path of war — Dunkirk, Benghazi, Mersa Matruh, Pearl Harbor, a harrowing lesson in geography.

Three miles up the road a rationed Nelson was doing its best to keep up the spirits of its people. A Salem Sunday School group had rambled to Lumb Spout, a waterfall above the village of Trawden, where "great excitement prevailed" when a gentleman's umbrella fell into the ravine. Nimble walkers retrieved it. The brolly was wet but as someone remarked "what is that to an umbrella". They were momentous times.

Dad had become At Homes secretary booking concert parties and staring into the mist for their arrival. Some optimist had risked recruiting me to play Sing Sing in the pantomime *Aladdin*. Santa Claus, recorded under his alternative name, had presented each child in the primary department with a big bag of sweets. The recording scribe believed that "he must have received some extra coupons from the Ministry of Food".

Meanwhile Nelson Corporation had taken up farming for victory and in 1943 was keeping cattle and planning for thirty sheep to be grazed on Nelson football ground. As the flock was parting with its winter coat in the spring of 1944 I would reach eighteen and be thought old enough to hamper the war effort more directly. His Majesty invited me into his Navy. The formative years, founded on a warm family, chapel and community, were to lead into another role, new settings, at home and abroad.

CHAPTER
THIRTY-ONE

A Past Revisited

Never go back, they say. After writing notes on a Pennine childhood and beyond I *do* go back to Tum Hill and find the face of time disguised. Old tracks, which took me home from school to farm near to where the Puffing Billy train steamed to a pause for passengers, have been lost under a housing scheme. A successor strikes up the side of a newer school than ours and after one or two fields I reach hawthorns and am stopped in my homecoming by a golf course.

Golfers are swinging to holes on what used to be Dad's lower meadow. A path crosses but nothing seems to go uphill. A woman walking a dog registers my geographical confusion. The golfers wouldn't mind, she suggests, if I follow a wall up the edge of their course. Nor should they mind. This was once a well-used path. Even so, I feel a twinge of the intruder as I sneak up it again to discover a familiar old lane, the straight-as-a-die lane from the top of town to our neighbour's farm and then on to ours. Bill Thornton's field on one side of the lane has grown bricks and mortar. The opposite side is also laid to golfing. Half expecting to hear a shout of "Fore!" I turn towards our neighbour's Gib Hill Farm. Like Brigadoon it has vanished but in its case never to reappear. Farmhouse, outbuildings and land have gone under golf drives. I pass its memory, listening for echoes of the Bather family, mumble against the cosmetics of time. The short twisty brow is here but a well, nourished from a ravine, has gone. The stile to a stiff slope down which we sledged to the gamble of a ducking in a stream is besieged by tarmac rubble, a heartbreak relieved only by pink dog roses in bloom.

Near the footings of Tum Hill a colour-washed cottage which sheltered below our farm has also disappeared. Here stands our farmhouse. Correction! Here stands our farmhouse in disguise. The frame persists but our old home has been extended, restored and given a new stone face. Barn, shippon and stable are no more. A garage stands where our hens laid warm brown eggs. A stone-walled track to the top pasture, modest as ever, is strangled by grass and brambles. A croft sprouts hawthorns and wild roses and is gay in its abandon. Even the word gay has been reinvented for another use.

Our hen cabins have gone and so has the ancient pigsty from the creepy hollow. A tarmac track continues to new housing and to the former home of the two Bills immediately below the summit. Tracks to the hill with coltsfoot, daisy, clover and buttercups are as remembered with tumbling walls, thistles and nettles and, as I approach, a couple of disturbed grouse. Great-grandfather, the unwanted boy from the train who knelt to pray within sight of where I now stand, would find little changed on top. It still offers wide-angle views of

Pendle, Boulsworth, the Yorkshire hills, Hameldon and beyond. Standing here with a solitary cropping Friesian cow, I recall our own tiny "herd". Here, too, a bank manager friend used to pass below the hill on his way to bank the hardearned coins of Colne, walking by choice for the exercise. The Friesian breed is out of keeping with the past. The bank manager lived to be a hundred.

The Colne-Nelson boundary has been built up and the towns, ancient and modern, have merged with smaller communities under the name Pendle. Nelson is isolated from through traffic which hums by on the M65 into congestion in Colne. Once you could probably hear the creak of pedals between the towns but now the valley growls with vehicles. Crossing the road is a risk and residents can't always park outside their own homes. Asda has come. Mills have closed. The town which welcomed Learie Constantine, one of the first black men regularly seen hereabouts, has adopted a huge Asian community. Salem chapel has gone, its fellowship merged with another congregation in new premises. Almost within earshot of the old hymn-singing a mosque lifts its green dome to the Pennine sky. A "megaphone" voice, like a call from the clouds, calls Muslim men to prayer. The muezzin at his post. My old newspaper still circulates here under the name *Lancashire Evening Telegraph* and, more personally, my son Peter is news editor of the *Nelson Leader/Colne Times* series of newspapers. My daughter Sandy visits regularly with her family from Southport, as do my wife Renée and I from Lathom.

From the old Iron Age fort I take the rutted track in Dad's top pasture, unclaimed by the golfers and still not much to write home about. Here stands the first pylon to power our oil-lit home. The straight lane on which I cycled for fish and chips has the old hump which tested boy and bicycle and I ask whether you could leave a cycle unlocked outside a shop today. Postwar housing keeps the farm names fragrant — New Gib Hill Road. Marsden Hall Farm, which supplied Dad's milk, survives but not as a farm. Walton Lane, our alternative sledge run in safer times, leads down to two stone lions at the park entrance. Inside the park where I used to play in potting sheds with Norman, son of the park manager, little seems to have changed though I hear of restoration plans for the old Marsden Hall and replica Roman bath and other needed improvements.

Nelson Secondary School, under a new name, shows up. Two youths are outside. "I used to go here," I venture. They eye me as the dinosaur I am. A silence hangs between us. I wait. "S'allreight in'it," one says.

I walk on past the school's tennis courts and a grassy bank down which boys have rolled or been rolled through the years and reflect on the news that a new "super school" is planned in the grounds. After seventy-six years of instruction the old building is to be demolished. A two-car diesel train glides by on the railway line below. I'm in the present time. To visit it with outdated maps is to meet the unexpected.

The blurred image of a Walls ice-cream man on his stop-me-and-buy-one tricycle is only an illusion.

187